THE
CORBETT
ALMANAC

Cameron McNeish

NEIL WILSON PUBLISHING • GLASGOW

© Cameron McNeish 1994

Published by Neil Wilson Publishing Ltd
309 The Pentagon Centre
36 Washington Street
GLASGOW G3 8AZ
Tel: 041-221-1117
Fax: 041-221-5363

The moral right of the author has been asserted.

A catalogue record for this book is available from the
British Library.
ISBN 1-897784-14-7.

Typeset in 8.5 on 9pt Times New Roman by
Face To Face Design Services, Glasgow.

Printed in Scotland by Scotprint, Musselburgh.

Also published by NWP:

The Best Hillwalking in Scotland
by *Cameron McNeish*
£14.95, ISBN 1-897784-06-6

The Munro Almanac
by *Cameron McNeish*
£6.99, ISBN 1-897784-01-5

Contents

Introduction

The Munros have become respectable. With the list of 'Munroists' now well over one thousand, and countless thousands more still tramping over the 3000-footers it seems that a new breed of hillgoer has evolved over the past decade. In the past there were hillwalkers or indeed mountaineers, who were in nodding acquaintance with the Munro list and who, from time to time, would make a note of the Munros they had climbed. Usually, such hillgoers would also be climbers, scramblers and perhaps even ski-tourers and at some stage in their career there would be a casual tallying up of the Munro ticks. Inevitably, if the list was in excess of 200 or so, there would a mild stimulus to make some kind of effort to 'tidy up' the remaining 77 hills. It wasn't, if you pardon the apparent elitism, something to make much of an effort over. In the hillgoing world there weren't many kudos to be gained from being a 'Munroist'.

Kudos are still in short supply, but the publication of Munros guidebooks, and even a television series, have prompted a new awareness of the Munro game. From being a part of something greater, it has grown into an activity in its own right!

A question often asked is this — what does one do when all the Munros have been climbed? The great Louis Armstrong was once asked by a journalist what it was that he got out of jazz? Satchmo looked at that man and said, 'Man! If you gotta ask a question like that you'll nevah get to know.' The Munro question is the same — it's usually asked by people who don't understand the hill game — who'll never understand. But one possible answer to it, and one that is being answered by an increasing number of hillwalkers is, 'the Corbetts'.

There are 221 Corbetts in Scotland. These are the hills between 2500 feet and 2999 feet, first collated by John Rooke Corbett, a member of the Scottish Mountaineering Club. He was a district valuer based in Bristol and was an enthusiastic and active member of the SMC, serving on the committee between the wars. He was also a founder member of the Rucksack Club. Like so many enthusiasts since, he must have travelled many thousands of miles in his countless forays to the Highlands from his base south of the Border. Astonishingly, he not only completed the Munros and Tops in 1930, but went on to climb all of Scotland's hills over 2000 feet!

Corbett didn't in fact publish his list of 2500-foot mountains. After his death his sister passed his list on to the SMC Guide Book general editor, who decided it was worthy of publication, so it was included in Munros Tables under, 'Other Tables of Lesser Heights'.

Corbett's list differed from the Munros in that it was much stricter in terms of what constituted a separate mountain. (There has always been much speculation and discussion about the criteria for deciding what separates a Munro 'top' from a 'mountain'). Corbett insisted on a re-ascent of 500 feet on all sides, between each listed hill and any neighbouring one, which means that the separation between the Corbetts is much more clearly defined than the Munros. The Corbetts therefore, are quite distinct and separate hills, making them much more individualistic.

Where you can often climb three or four, or on one occasion seven Munros in one single walk, there are few Corbett groups where you can climb more than two or three on a single walk.

There is still a temptation to regard the Corbetts as inferior hills. They most definitely are not. When you consider the likes of the Cobbler, Foinaven, Quinag, Ben Loyal, Fuar Tholl, Garbh Bheinn of Ardgour and Ben Aden you realise that what they may lack in a few feet they undoubtedly gain in sheer character. They are among the finest hills in the country! And the real bonus is that the Corbetts will take you into parts of Scotland where there are no Munros. The Isles of Rum, Harris and Jura for example. Or the wonderfully rough and wild Ardgour or Applecross or Galloway. Another advantage is that so many of the Corbetts offer superb views of the bigger Munros, views that you can't quite appreciate when looking down from the Munros themselves.

Notes on using this book

I have used the same area boundaries as those listed in *The Munro Almanac*. However, there are some areas where there are Corbetts, and no Munros, notably Southern Scotland and Ardgour, so I have noted these areas as Section 1(a) and Section 22(a). This means that there is a consistency between *The Munro Almanac* and *The Corbett Almanac*. Likewise, there are several areas where there are Munros but no Corbetts, and in these situations I have put the sections together, eg, Sections 6/7, Killin Hills and Sections 14/15, Loch Ericht and Drumochter.

Each section contains information on accommodation, public transport to and within the section area, the height and grid reference of each summit, the meaning and pronunciation of each hill name and details of the most straightforward ascent, including approximate times, distances and ascent climbed.

Contour line measurements in the route descriptions have been given in metres in line with the current 1:50000 Ordnance Survey (OS) maps. For distances on the hill both miles and kilometres are quoted as well as feet (ft) and metres (m) where appropriate. I suspect most hill walkers still tend to think in terms of miles and feet ascended — indeed much of the character of the Munros or Corbetts would be lost if we referred to them as over 914.4m or 762m!

The route descriptions, as in *The Munro Almanac*, are not meant to offer a step by step account of how to climb each mountain, but only to give a rough outline of what I have found to be the best line of ascent and descent. Many will undoubtedly disagree with some of the routes I recommend, but I have tried to balance the need for longer multi-top expeditions with shorter day trips. There are some areas, such as the Glenshee area, where two or three quite separate hills can be climbed in a day, provided the walker has transport to drive between them. The descriptions should only be used as a guide, in conjunction with the appropriate Ordnance Survey maps.

Access

It has always been understood that in Scotland the hillwalker or mountaineer has enjoyed a moral right of freedom-to-roam in wild places, provided that is accompanied by good countryside manners and respect for those other activities which also make use of wild land areas, ie, grouse shooting and deer stalking. This de facto freedom to roam must be safeguarded for sadly, there is a growing number of landowners who are worried about the increased numbers of walkers on the hills and who are anxious to see a change in the law regarding access.

At present, the law in Scotland says that trespass has been committed by a person who goes on to land owned or occupied by another without that person's consent and without having a right to do so. But, a simple trespass is not enshrined in statute as a criminal offence, so there can't be a prosecution. The owner or occupier of the property must either obtain interdict, (i.e., a court ruling that the trespass must not happen again) or, if damage to property has occurred, to raise an action for damages. Additionally, a 'trespasser' may be asked by a landowner or occupier to leave the property and in the event of that person refusing to leave, the owner or occupier has the right to use 'reasonable force' to make him or her leave. Such 'reasonable force' has never been defined!

However, there is a widely held public acceptance that walkers and mountaineers are more or less free to roam the upland areas of Scotland without undue restriction, and any impingement on that moral right would undoubtedly create public outcry. At the time of writing Scottish Natural Heritage has published a discussion document on access and is awaiting comment. In recent years there has been much dialogue between hillgoers and the Scottish Landowners Federation in a search for mutual understanding and tolerance and other than in a very few well publicised areas there is good harmony between the two groups.

Most estates in the Highlands are involved in deer stalking and ask hillgoers to respect the stag shooting season which runs from 20th August to 20th October.

During this time there are many areas of upland Scotland which are not affected by stalking, like those areas owned by the National Trust for Scotland and many Scottish Natural Heritage reserves. I have listed local telephone numbers of estates, however, so that you can find out for yourself where stalking is taking place. Often a chat with a gamekeeper or the factor will result in a good compromise which will be satisfactory to both parties.

But please bear in mind that estates often earn a substantial amount of their annual income from stalking, and there often has to be a compromise. The alternative to stalking in many areas could well be something more unpleasant, like forestry. Dialogue and mutual respect and understanding is the only way forward.

1(a) South Scotland

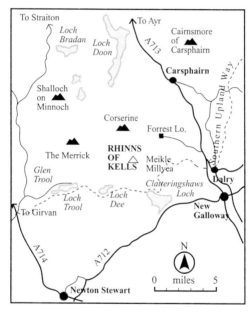

Suggested Base	Newton Stewart or Moffat.
Accommodation	Hotels, guest houses, b&b at Newton Stewart and Glen Trool village, Moffat, Dalmellington and Tweedsmuir. Youth hostels at Minnigaff, Newton Stewart and Kendoon. Camp sites at Caldons near Loch Trool, Moffat.
Public Transport	Rail: Stations at Dumfries, Lockerbie and Stranraer. Buses: Regular services between Dumfries and Newton Stewart and the

Newton Stewart to Ayr service
calls at Glen Trool village. There
are also services from Dumfries
and Lockerbie to Moffat.

Mountain: Merrick, 2766ft/843m.
Map: OS Sheet 77: GR 428855.
Translation: the branched finger.
Pronunciation: as spelt.
Access Point: Upper car park at end of public road in
Glen Trool.
Distance/ascent: 8mls/2500ft; 13km/762m.
Approx Time: 4-6 hours.
Route: Follow the path on the W bank of the Buchan
Burn. At Culsharg bothy a path runs through the forest
in a NW direction, then N to a wall which leads to the
top of Benyellary. Follow this wall over Benyellary in
a N direction before bearing NE to a high col. Climb
the rock studded upper slopes to the summit. An alter-
native descent is by way of the col between Loch Enoch
and the Buchan Burn, then over the Rig of Loch Enoch
and Buchan Hill back to Loch Trool.
Stalking Information: Forestry Commission.
Tel: 0671-46208.

Mountain: Shalloch on Minnoch, 2543ft/775m.
Map: OS Sheet: 77 GR 405907.
Translation: the heel of the Minnoch ridge.
Pronunciation: as spelt.
Access Point: Bell Memorial car park, GR 353907.
Distance/ascent: 8mls/1700ft; 13km/518m.
Approx Time: 3-5 hours.
Route: Follow the burn to Laglanny where a forestry
road is picked up. This leads to a ruined farm WSW of
the hill. From the farm follow the Shalloch Burn, which
is crossed about a quarter of a mile beyond the farm. A
firebreak follows a tributary burn and this leads onto
the grassy W ridge of Shalloch on Minnoch. Ascend
this ridge to the summit. An alternative descent, making a good circular walk, descends S from Shalloch on

Minnoch over Nick of Carlach, Tarfessock, Carmeddie Brae to Kirrieroch Hill before descending the W ridge of the latter hill through the forest back to the road.
Stalking Information: Forestry Commission.
Tel: 0671-46208.

Mountain: Corserine, 2669ft/814m.
Map: OS Sheet 77: GR 498871.
Translation: the crossing of the ridges.
Pronunciation: *corsereen.*
Access Point: Car park near Forrest Lodge, GR 552865.
Distance/ascent: 7½mls/2350ft; 12km/716m.
Approx Time: 4-6 hours.
Route: A road leaves the A713 at Polharrow Bridge and leads to a car park close to Forrest Lodge. Continue on the road following the south bank of the Polharrow Burn. Pass Fore Bush and shortly after leave the road and go along the south shores of Loch Harrow. At the west end of the loch a firebreak in the trees leads uphill and onto the North Gairy Top of Corserine. Ascend the ridge and reach the broad grassy summit.

A different descent can be enjoyed by following the line of the Rhinns of Kells to the SSE, over the tops of Millfire, Milldown and Meikle Millyea. From the latter top, descend the NE ridge, leaving it in an eastwards direction on the lower slopes. From here, follow the edge of the forest in an eastwards direction to a stile. Cross it and follow the firebreak to the forest road, which in turn leads back to Forrest Lodge.
Stalking Information: Forrest Estate.
Tel: 06443-230.

Mountain: Cairnsmore of Carsphairn, 2614ft/797m.
Map: OS Sheet 77: GR 594980.
Translation: unknown.
Pronunciation: as spelt.
Access Point: A713, close to the bridge over the Water of Deugh, GR 557945.
Distance/ascent: 6½ mls/2150ft; 11kms/655m.
Approx Time: 4-6 hours.

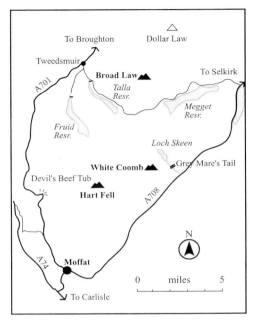

Route: Start close to the Green Well of Scotland, just east of the bridge over the Water of Deugh. Go through a gate by the roadside house and follow the track on the east bank of the Water of Deugh. Pass a shed, and shortly after crossing the Benloch Burn leave the track and take to the open south western slopes of Willieanna. Climb to the summit, follow the broad ridge to Dunool, follow the ridge eastwards then NNE to Black shoulder from where a short (1km) and easy ascent takes you to the summit cairn and trig point of Cairnsmore. Descend by Cairnsmore's west ridge, leaving it to cross the Polsue Burn from where you can pick up the track from the A713.

Stalking Information: Holm of Daltallachon.
Tel: 06446-208.

The Grey Mare's tail on the way to White Coomb

Mountain: Hart Fell, 2651ft/808m.
Map: OS Sheet 78: GR 113135.
Translation: hill of the small deer.
Pronunciation: as spelt.
Access Point: The Moffat to Ericstane road, GR 076104.
Distance/ascent: 6 mls/2000ft; 10kms/610m.
Approx Time: 4-6 hours.
Route: A signpost points the way to Hartfell Spa, 2½mls/6km from Moffat on the Ericstane road at the red corrugate community hall. Follow the path to the beehive shaped building which houses the spa. Climb to the ridge on your right above the spa, and follow it easily to the summit of Hart Fell. Descend the way you came, (directly down the SW ridge ommitting the Spa) or alternatively, continue WNW down into a deep bealach between Hart Fell and Whitehope Knowe. Ascend Whitehope, cross the tops of Chalk Rig Edge and Great Hill to reach the Devil's Beef Tub. From there a good track leads to Corehead, and then back to Ericstane. (Hart Fell can be climbed in conjunction with White Coomb by way of Rotten Bottom, but you will require two cars. Rotten Bottom isn't particularly recommended!).
Stalking Information: Economic Forestry.
Tel: 0450-78353.

Mountain: White Coomb, 2696ft/822m.
Map: OS Sheet 79: GR 163151.
Translation: white corrie.
Pronunciation: *white coom.*
Access Point: A708, NTS car park at foot of Grey Mare's Tail.
Distance/ascent: 4½mls/2000ft; 7km/610m.
Approx Time: 3-4 hours.
Route: Leave the NTS car park and take the footpath which follows the NE bank of the Tail Burn. Follow the path with spectacular views of the Grey Mare's Tail, to above the falls where the path levels off. Cross the burn well above the falls and head westwards, over Upper Tarnberry. An old wall, with a path beside it, leads up Rough Craigs, avoiding the steepest slopes. Follow the wall, but note that it doesn't lead directly to the summit cairn but passes it 100m to the north. Descend north for half a kilometre, and drop down the steep slopes beside the Midlaw Burn to Loch Skeen. From there follow the footpath alongside the Tail Burn, past the falls to the car park below.
Stalking Information: NTS, no restrictions.

Mountain: Broad Law, 2756ft/840m.
Map: OS Sheet 72: GR 146235.
Translation: wide hillside.
Pronunciation: as spelt.
Access Point: The Megget Stone (GR151203) on the minor road from Tweedsmuir to St. Mary's Loch.
Distance/ascent: 4mls/1200ft; 7km/365m.
Approx Time: 2-4 hours.
Route: Leave the road by the Megget Stone and follow the fence which leads up the broad ridge northwards. Go over the minor tops of Fans Law and Cairn Law and follow the long, gently undulating rise to Broad Law itself. From Broad Law another broad and undulating ridge leads NE over Cramalt Craig, Dun Law to Dollar Law, a worthwhile extension to the easy walk up Broad Law. Return the same way, or if transport can

be arranged follow the radio mast maintenance road down by the lines of the Glenheurie Rig and Hearthstane Burn to the Crook Inn.

Stalking Information: Wemyss and March Estate, Norman Douglas.

Tel: 0750-8206, or the shepherd on 0750-4236.

1 The Arrochar Alps

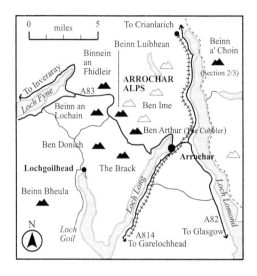

Suggested Base Accommodation	Arrochar. Hotels, guest houses and b&b at Arrochar, Ardlui, Cairndow, and Inveraray. Youth hostels at Arrochar (Ardgarten), Balloch, (Loch Lomond), Inveraray, and Inverbeg. Camping/caravan sites at Ardgarten, Ardlui, Arrochar, Balloch, Inveraray and Luss.
Public Transport	Rail: London to Fort William and Glasgow to Oban and Fort William. Stations at Arrochar and Ardlui. Buses: Arrochar, Glen Croe, Glen Kinglas, and Cairndow can all be reached by bus from Glasgow.

Mountain: Beinn Bheula, 2570ft/783m.
Map: OS Sheet 56: GR 155983.
Translation: hill of the ford.
Pronunciation: *ben vyoola.*
Access Point: Lettermay, GR 187002.
Distance/ascent: 6mls/2440ft; 10km/744m.
Approx Time: 3-5 hours.
Route: Begin at Lettermay on Loch Goil-side and take the Forestry Commission road up the glen for about a mile in a westerly direction. After a mile, turn left on a path which leads on an upwards traverse through the pines to the outflow of Lochan nan Cnaimh. From here a fainter path, marked at intervals by posts, leads up to a broad bealach. From the bealach, climb the slopes in a NW direction, avoiding the steep crags and then strike northwards over the twin-topped Creag Sgoilte and along the broad grassy ridge to the trig point on Beinn Bheula. Descend by the rough NE ridge to the outflow of the Curra Lochain and follow the forestry track back to Lettermay.

NB: The forestry track from Lettermay is not shown on the OS First Series maps.
Stalking Information: Forestry Commission.
Tel: 03012-597.

Mountain: Ben Donich, 2795ft/852m.
              The Brack, 2597ft/792m.
Map: OS Sheet 56: GR 218044, GR 245031.
Translation: brown hill, speckled hill (possibly).
Pronunciation: *ben dawnich, the braack.*
Access Point: Forestry Commission office in Glen Croe, GR 270037.
Distance/ascent: 9½mls/2800ft; 16km/853m.
Approx Time: 5-7 hours.
Route: From the Forestry Commission office in Glen Croe take the forestry road which runs up the glen below the N face of The Brack. After about 2½mls/4km take the path which turns S to the Bealach Dubh-lic above the headwaters of the Donich Water, or Allt Coire

---

Ben Arthur, affectionately known as the Cobbler

Odhair. From the bealach climb the N ridge of The Brack, and return the same way. Ascend Ben Donich by its broad and rather featureless E ridge.

An alternative route, if transport can be arranged, is to climb Ben Donich by its N ridge from near the Rest and Be Thankful, descend its E ridge to the Bealach Dubh-lic, ascend the N ridge of The Brack, descending by its SW ridge into the Coilessan Glen. Follow the footpath E and SE down the Coilessan Glen to Loch Long and then N to Ardgarten.

Stalking Information: Forestry Commission.
Tel: 03012-597.

Mountain: The Cobbler (Ben Arthur), 2899ft/884m.
Map: OS Sheet 56: GR 259059.
Translation: Possibly from King Arthur, the Cobbler refers to the shape of the hill which is said to resemble a cobbler working at his last.
Pronunciation: as spelt.
Access Point: A83, by the Buttermilk Burn, GR 287042.
Distance/ascent: 5mls/2500ft; 8km/762m.
Approx Time: 4-6 hours.
Route: Leave the A83 where the Buttermilk Burn, (Allt a'Bhalachain) runs below the road into Loch Long. Follow the path through the woods beside the stream. (The stream bed itself offers a delightful, scrambling route up the hillside in times of drought.) Once free of

the trees continue on the path and cross to the eastern
bank of the river by the dam to pick up the track that
comes up from Succoth. Follow the track NW, past the
Narnain Boulders and up into the SE corrie. The path
continues to climb steadily up to the obvious bealach
between the central and north peaks of the mountain.
On the bealach turn immediately right and follow the
well worn path onto the north peak. Return to the
bealach and continue on the path to the rocky central
peak, the summit of the mountain. Some rock climbing
skills are called for here. The way to the summit isn't
all that evident; you must crawl through a gash between
the two main summit rocks. Once through the slit follow the traversing ledge which runs leftwards around
the back of the rock where a couple of obvious holds
lift you onto the summit platform. Return the same way.
Stalking Information: Forestry Commission.
Tel: 03012-597.

Mountain: Beinn Luibhean, 2815ft/858m.
Map: OS Sheet 56: GR 243079.
Translation: hill of the small plant.
Pronunciation: *ben loo-ee-ven* .
Access Point: A83, 200m south of the bridge over the
Kinglas Water.
Distance/ascent: 4mls/2220ft; 6km/677m.
Approx Time: 3-5 hours.
Route: Leave the A83 at a point about 200m south of
the old bridge over the Kinglas water near a ruined cottage. Pass the cottage and follow a well trodden path
up the SW bank of the burn which falls from the Bealach
a'Mhargaidh, the bealach between Beinn Luibhean and
the Munro, Beinn Ime. Follow the burn to the flat ex-
panse of the bealach, turn due W and climb the broad
and rocky E ridge of Beinn Luibhean to the summit
cairn.

This Corbett is obviously well placed to climb with
Beinn Ime. Return to your starting point from the
Bealach a'Mhargaidh.

Stalking Information: Forestry Commission.
Tel: 03012-597.

Mountain: Beinn an Lochain, 2975ft/907m.
Map: OS Sheet 56: GR 218079.
Translation: hill of the small loch.
Pronunciation: ben an lochen.
Access Point: A83, 200m south of the bridge over the Kinglas Water. (As for Beinn Luibhean).
Distance/ascent: 4½mls/2200ft; 7km/670m.
Approx Time: 2-4 hours.
Route: Follow the stream which issues from the N of Loch Restil and cross it near the head of the loch. Walk in a NW direction to gain access to the mountain's NE ridge by means of an obvious wide, grassy gully. Follow the interesting and rocky ridge over a number of false summits to the summit cairn. Continue S over the summit to the small subsidiary southern summit. Continue SSW, avoiding the crags overlooking the Rest and Be Thankful, before dropping down steep grassy slopes to the top of the B828 Lochgoilhead road. Follow the A83 back to the starting point.
Stalking Information: Forestry Commission.
Tel: 03012-597.

Mountain: Binnein an Fhidhleir, 2680ft/817m.
Map: OS Sheet 56/50: GR 230109.
Translation: peak of the fiddler.
Pronunciation: beenyan an yeelar.
Access Point: A83, west of the bridge over Kinglas water.
Distance/ascent: 4 mls/2200ft; 6km/670m.
Approx Time: 2-4 hours.
Route: Leave the A83 in Glen Kinglas just W of the bridge over Kinglas Water. Climb the steep slopes in a N direction to gain the mountain's broad SE ridge. The small crags higher up this ridge are easy to avoid, as are those which surround the summit. From the summit, unnamed on the map, follow the broad ridge due

W to the lower, but named summit of Binnein an Fhidhleir, from where steep slopes to the S lead back to the A83 in Glen Kinglas.

(The Scottish Mountaineering Club have proposed that the 817m summit of this hill be named Stob Coire Creagach, after the hill's NE corrie, but there is no reason why the whole mountain can't be named Binnein an Fhidhleir.)

Stalking Information: Hydro Board.
Tel: 03014-245.

2/3 Crianlarich, Tyndrum and Bridge of Orchy

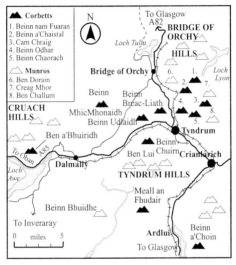

▲▲ **Corbetts**
1. Beinn nam Fuaran
2. Beinn a'Chaistal
3. Cam Chraig
4. Beinn Odhar
5. Beinn Chaorach

△△ **Munros**
6. Ben Dorain
7. Creag Mhor
8. Ben Challum

CRUACH HILLS

BRIDGE OF ORCHY HILLS

To Glasgow A82

Loch Tulla

Loch Lyon

Bridge of Orchy

Beinn MhicMhonaidh

Beinn Breac-Liath

Beinn Udlaidh

Ben a'Bhuiridh

To Oban A85

Dalmally

Loch Awe

Beinn Chuirn

Ben Lui

Tyndrum

Crianlarich

TYNDRUM HILLS

Meall an Fhudair

Beinn Bhuidhe

To Inveraray

Ardlui

To Glasgow

Beinn a'Choin

0   miles   5

Suggested Base Accommodation	Crianlarich or Tyndrum. Hotels, guest houses and b&b at Crianlarich and Tyndrum. Youth hostel at Crianlarich and private bunk house at Bridge of Orchy. Caravan site at Tyndrum and camping/caravan site in Glen Dochart.
Public Transport	Rail: Crianlarich, Tyndrum and Bridge of Orchy are on the West Highland Line, London/Glasgow to Fort William. Crianlarich and Tyndrum are also on the Glasgow to Oban line. Buses: Glasgow to Fort William or Oban for Crianlarich or Tyndrum.

Mountain: Beinn a'Choin, 2525ft/770m.
Map: OS Sheet 56: GR 354130.
Translation: hill of the dogs.
Pronunciation: ben-a-kon.
Access Point: A82, Inverarnan.
Distance/ascent: 10mls/2900ft; 16kms/884m.
Approx Time: 6-8 hours.
Route: Leave the Inverarnan Inn and follow the A82 N to the West Highland Way signpost. Cross the bridge over the River Falloch and follow the route of the WHW by Beinglas for about 2½mls/4km to the bothy at Doune. Leave the footpath and climb steep slopes W to the summit of Stob nan Eighrach. From here, follow the ridge S to Maol an Fhithich and SE to the summit slopes of Beinn a'Choin. Return by way of Stob nan Eighrach. For an alternative descent continue N then NE to spiky Ben Ducteach, then NNE for about 3km to the Ben Glas Burn. Descend W by the waterfall to Beinglas and Inverarnan.
Stalking Information: Glenfalloch Estate.
Tel: 03014-229.

Mountain: Meall an Fhudair, 2508ft/764m.
Map: OS Sheet 50: GR 271192.
Translation: gunpowder hill.
Pronunciation: myowl an foo-tar.
Access Point: A82 opposite Glenfalloch Farm.
Distance/ascent: 8 mls/2640ft; 13km/805m.
Approx Time: 4-6 hours.
Route: A Hydro Electric Board road leaves the A82 opposite Glenfalloch Farm and zig zags its way up the lower E slopes of Troisgeach. After a series of zig zags, the road joins another Hydro road which contours round the hill in a SSW direction. Leave this road, and take to the slopes in a W direction, climbing directly to the summit of Troisgeach. Continue in a NW direction to Meall nan Caora, then WSW past an assortment of small lochans to the Corbett, Meall an Fhudair. Descend the steep slopes to the SE and drop down into the Lairig

---

Arnan. Continue down the pass and pick up the Hydro road again which should be followed back to the zig zags above Glenfalloch.
Stalking Information: Glenfalloch Estate.
Tel: 03014-229.

Mountain: Beinn Chuirn, 2887ft/880m.
Map: OS Sheet 50: GR 281292.
Translation: cairn hill.
Pronunciation: ben a chooirn.
Access Point: Tyndrum.
Distance/ascent: 7½mls/2300ft; 12km/701m.
Approx Time: 4-6 hours.
Route: Take the track behind the lower railway station in Tyndrum and follow it for some 3.5km to Cononish farm. Continue past the farm for a kilometre or so before taking to the SE slopes of Beinn Chuirn beyond the goldmining explorations. Continue climbing the grassy slopes in a NW direction above the Eas Anie falls and up the broad SE ridge of Beinn Chuirn to the summit. An ancient fence crosses the summit just N of the cairn. Descend the same way.
Stalking Information: Auchessan Estate.
Tel: 08383-518.

Mountain: Beinn a'Bhuiridh, 2942ft/897m.
Map: OS Sheet 50: GR 094283.
Translation: Hill of stag's roaring.
Pronunciation: byn a voo-ree.
Access Point: Falls of Cruachan, GR 078268.
Distance/ascent: 4mls/2500ft; 6km/762m.
Approx Time: 2-4 hours.
Route: Climb steeply up the path beside the Allt Cruachab to the Cruachan dam access road. From the dam, climb ENE to the summit. Return the same way. A longer, and more satisfying circuit, begins at the junction of the A85 and the B8077. This route follows the ridges which surround Coire Ghlais. From the A85, climb the SE slopes of Monadh Driseag, and continue WNW to Beinn a'Bhuiridh. Descend NE and cross the

Larig Torran then follow the lines of cliffs ENE and E
for 1.5km before descending to the Allt Coire Ghlais
and a return to the starting point.
Stalking Information: Castles Farm.
Tel: 08382-247.

Mountain: Beinn Mhic-Mhonaidh, 2610ft/796m.
Map: OS Sheet 50: GR 208349.
Translation: hill of the son of the moor.
Pronunciation: byn vic voana.
Access Point: B8074, GR 243321.
Distance/ascent: 8mls/2400ft; 13km/732m.
Approx Time: 4-6 hours.
Route: Cross the forestry bridge just below the Eas
Urchaidh, (Fall of Orchy) and follow the track beside
the Allt Broighleachan till it comes to an end. A track
crosses the burn and forks, so take the left fork and
follow the track to the edge of the trees. Pass the ruined
shielings of Airigh Chailleach and climb the steep S
facing slopes to gain the summit ridge. Climb the ridge
in a NE direction to the summit. Return the same way.
Stalking Information: Craig Estate.
Tel: 08382-213.

Mountain: Beinn Udlaidh, 2755ft/840m
               Beinn Bhreac-liath, 2633ft/803m.
Map: OS Sheet 50: GR 280333, GR 303339.
Translation: dark, or gloomy, hill, speckled grey hill.
Pronunciation: byn oot-lay, byn vrechk lee-a.
Access Point: Invergaunan, B8074.
Distance/ascent: 8mls/3000ft; 13km/914m.
Approx Time: 5-7 hours.
Route: Leave the B8074 at Invergaunan and follow the
Allt Ghamhnain for a short distance before bearing S
to gain the broad N ridge of Beinn Udlaidh. From the
summit continue S for a short distance then due E to
descend to a broad bealach between Udlaidh and the
steep slopes of Beinn Bhreac-Liath. From the bealach
climb Bhreac-Liath in a NE direction to its flat sum-
mit. Return to Invergaunan by the long N ridge.
Stalking Information: C.Macdonald, Auch Estate.
Tel: 08384-233.

Beinn a'Chasteil near Auch

Mountain: Beinn Odhar, 2955ft/901m
Beinn Chaorach, 2685ft/818m
Cam Chreag, 2900ft/884m
Beinn nam Fuaran, 2645ft/806m
Beinn a'Chaisteil, 2907ft/886m.
Map: OS Sheet 50; GR338339, GR359328, GR375346, GR361381, GR348364.
Translation: dun-coloured hill, sheep hill, crooked crag, hill of the well, hill of the castle.
Pronunciation: *byn oo-er, byn choer-ach, caam craick, byn nam foo-uran, byn a chastyal.*
Access Point: A82, GR 329331.
Distance/ascent: 11mls/6500ft; 18kms/1981m.
Approx Time: 8-10 hours.
Route: This is probably the only group of Corbetts which contains 5 tops, and as such involves considerable ascent and descent. Leave the car at the parking space on the A82, drop down from the road onto the line of the West Highland Way and follow it to cross under the railway line. Climb the steep slopes of Beinn Odhar's SW ridge making use of an old mining track. After a while the ridge eases in steepness and you'll pass a small lochan. Climb from there to the summit cairn. Drop down the SE ridge to a small lochan, drained by the Allt Choire Dhuibh, then continue SE to the obvious bealach between Beinn Odhar and Beinn Chaorach. Climb Chaorach's steep flank can be climbed following the line of an electric fence, but this leads you onto the ridge about 200m N of the summit before

it turns N itself. Follow the broad NNE ridge for a kilometre to another bealach where there is a small wind
generator. From here follow the slopes NE then E up
Cam Chreag's broken and curving ridge to the summit
which sits at the head of a long broad summit ridge.
Descend now in a NNW direction, cross the Abhainn
Ghlas near its junction with the Allt a'Mhaim and climb
due N to the summit of Beinn nam Fuaran. Drop down
from the summit in a SW direction to cross a broad
peat hag ridden bealach and a long even pull up onto
the last top of the day, Beinn a'Chaisteil. The 883m
marked on the map is a spot height, and the cairn is
situated 100m N of the actual summit, just to confuse
you after a long day! Descend SE above Creagan Liatha
for 1.5 km before a steep descent drops you down into
Gleann Choillean where the track can be followed to
the Auch Gleann and the West Highland Way, which is
then followed back to the starting point.
Stalking Information: Auch Estate.
Tel: 08384-233.

4 Strathyre & Loch Earn

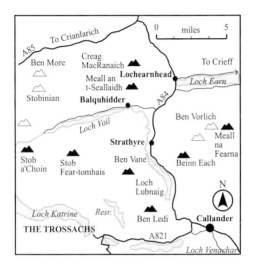

Suggested Base	Strathyre or Comrie.
Accommodation	Hotels, guest houses and b&b at Callander, Comrie, Crieff, Lochearnhead, St. Fillans and Strathyre. Camping sites at Callander and Crieff. Caravan/camping sites at Comrie. Youth hostels at Killin and Trossachs.
Public Transport	Rail: London, Glasgow and Edinburgh to Inverness. Connecting buses from stations at Perth and Stirling. Buses: Stirling to Crieff and Callander for ongoing connections. Both Crieff and Comrie can be reached by bus from Perth.

Mountain: Ben Ledi, 2883ft/879m
           Benvane, 2694ft /821m.
Map: OS Sheet 57: GR 562098, GR 535137.
Translation: God's hill, white hill.
Pronunciation: *byn ledy, bynvain.*
Access Point: A821, Brig o'Turk.
Distance/ascent: 12mls/3200ft; 19km/975m.
Approx Time: 6-8 hours.
Route: Leave Brig o'Turk and take the minor road which eventually leads to Glen Finglas Reservoir. Leave this road to take the track up Gleann Casaig and after 1½km take to the open W slopes of Ben Ledi. Climb W to the summit. From the cairn follow the ridge N to the Lochan nan Corp, then N and NW to Stuc Dhubh. Continue NW above the crags of Creag Chaoruinneach, then W and N to the summit of Benvane. To descend follow the long S ridge of Benvane back to Glen Finglas Reservoir and the road to Brig o'Turk.
Stalking Information: Milton of Callander Estate.
Tel: 0877-30162.

Mountain: Stob a'Choin, 2850ft/867m.
Map: OS Sheet 56: GR 417160.
Translation: dog peak.
Pronunciation: *stob a kon.*
Access Point: Inverlochlarig.
Distance/ascent: 6 mls/2500ft; 10km/762m.
Approx Time: 4-6 hours.
Route: Leave the Inverlochlarig Tourist Information Centre, and follow the road through Inverlochlarig itself. Continue past the buildings for about 1km to a footbridge which crosses to the S bank of the River Larig. Continue W beside the river for ½km to a sheepfold then follow the burn S up steep slopes, avoiding the broken crags of Amar Stob a' Choin on your right. Continue SW to the summit. Descend by Coire an Laoigh to Blaircreith.
Stalking Information: Inverlochlarig TIC.
Tel: 08774-232/249.

Mountain: Ceann na Baintighearna, (Stob Fear-
Tomhais), 2531ft/771m.
Map: OS Sheet 57: GR 474163.
Translation: her ladyship's head.
Pronunciation: *kyown na bantyeearna.*
Access Point: Ballimore Farm, GR 529175.
Distance/ascent: 7½mls/1800ft; 12km/549m.
Approx Time: 3-5 hours.
Route: Un-named on the OS map, the hill's name has
historically been taken from its rocky bluff which over-
looks Loch Doine in the north. However, the SMC have
chosen to call it by a Gaelic translation of a local name,
Stob Fear-tomhais, the surveyor's peak.

Ballimore Farm, 2¾mls/3km south of Balquhidder
offers a good starting point which avoids much of the
forestry. Cross the bridge over the Calair Burn and follow the right of way which eventually leads to Brig
o'Turk. Where the path begins to turn S continue W
across the river and climb the broad E ridge of Ceann
na Bainighearna. Follow the ridge over several bumps
to the triangulation pillar which gives the hill it's local
name. Descend the same way.
Stalking Information: Balquhidder Estate.
Tel: 08774-232/249.

Mountain: Beinn Each, 2667ft/813m.
Map: OS Sheet 57: GR 602158.
Translation: horse hill.
Pronunciation: *byn yech.*
Access Point: Glen Ample, GR 581136.
Distance/ascent: 4mls/2300ft; 6km/701m.
Approx Time: 3-4 hours.
Route: Leave the A84 at a lay-by on its N side and
follow the right of way track which climbs steeply NE
to Glen Ample. After a mile or so leave the track to
climb the steep SW slopes of Beinn Each to the sum-
mit.
Stalking Information: Glen Ample Estate.
Tel: 05673-202.

Mountain: Meall na Fearna, 2654ft/809m.
Map: OS Sheets 51/57: GR 651186.
Translation: hill of the alder.
Pronunciation: *myowl na fyaarna.*
Access Point: Ardvorlich, S side of Loch Earn.
Distance/ascent: 8mls/2150ft; 13km/655m.
Approx Time: 4-7 hours.
Route: Go through the east gate of Ardvorlich House and follow the road which shortly becomes a track S into Glen Vorlich. At a junction of paths continue left. About half a mile onwards follow the stream which comes down from the bealach between Ben Vorlich and Meall na Fearna. Follow the path beside the stream to the high point of the bealach. Leave the path and climb the slopes to the NE, avoiding the corrie to the south, to the un-named top at GR 643187. Turn SE over a shallow, peaty bealach, to the small summit cairn.
Stalking Information: Ardvorlich Estate.
Tel: 076485-260.

Mountain: Meall an t-Seallaidh, 2794ft/852m.
Map: OS Sheet 51: GR 542234.
Translation: hill of the sight.
Pronunciation: *myowl an tyalee.*
Access Point: Balquhidder.
Distance/ascent: 7mls/2300ft; 11km/701m.
Approx Time: 4-6 hours.
Route: Follow the right of way up Kirkton Glen which leaves Balquhidder beside the Auld Kirk, the burial place of Rob Roy. Please don't park in the church car park but beside the road to the south. Soon the path joins a forestry road and this should be followed NNW until it comes out of the trees near to the Lochan an Eireannaich. Double back now in an E direction over rough ground to gain the Cam Chreag ridge. Continue S along the summit ridge to the double top. The most northerly top, with the cairn, is thought to be the higher.
Stalking Information: Forestry Commission.
Tel: 08772-383.

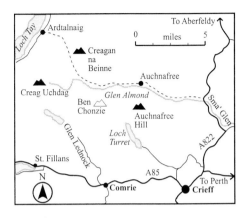

Mountain: Creag MacRanaich, 2654ft/809m.
Map: OS Sheet 51: GR 546256.
Translation: MacRainaich's hill.
Pronunciation: krayk mahkraneech.
Access Point: Car park in Glen Ogle, GR 557283.
Distance/ascent: 5mls/1700ft; 8km/518m.
Approx Time: 3-4 hours.
Route: Leave the car park in Glen Ogle, cross the road
and take to the hill just N of the forestry plantation be-
yond Loch Larig Eala. Climb the heathery slopes in
SW then S direction up the broad N ridge of Creag
MacRanaich. Follow the ridge to the summit.
Stalking Information: Forestry Commission.
Tel: 08772-383.
NB: Creag MacRanaich and Meall an t-Seallaidh can
be combined in one expedition by crossing the tricky
ground at the head of Gleann Dubh. Routes through the
crags can be easily found in good weather but can pose
some problems in poor visibility. A traverse of both
these hills requires some form of transport arrangement
to take you back to your starting point.

■■■■■■■■■■■■

Mountain: Creag Uchdag, 2883ft/879m
 Creagan na Beinne; 2913ft/888m.
Map: OS Sheet 51: GR 708323, GR 744369.
Translation: crag of the hollows, hill of the crags.
Pronunciation: krayk oochkak, kraykan na byn.
Access Point: Ardeonaig, GR 668358.
Distance/ascent: 15mls/3950ft; 24km/1204m.
Approx Time: 8-10 hours.
Route: Leave Ardeonaig and take the path on the E
side of the river which eventually leads over the Finglen
to Glen Lednock. From the top of the pass climb the
slopes due E following an old boundary fence. As the
slope steepens, flank slightly left to gain the Creag
Uchdag ridge. The summit lies at the E end of the short
ridge. Head N then E to skirt the corrie of Meall nan
Oighreag and descend from the 818m point to Dunan
at the head of Glen Almond. Head NE across bumpy
moraines to gain the broad S ridge of Creagan na Beinne.
Climb the ridge N to the summit. Descend W into
Gleann a'Chilleine and follow the path N to Ardtalnaig
on Loch Tay-side.
Stalking Information: Forestry Commission.
Tel: 0796-3437.

■■■■■■■■■■■■

Mountain: Auchnafree Hill, 2589ft/789m.
Map: OS Sheet 52: GR 808308.
Translation: hill of the deer forest field.
Pronunciation: och na free-ya.
Access Point: Loch Turret dam.
Distance/ascent: 7mls/1300ft; 11 km/396m.
Approx Time: 3-4 hours.
Route: Leave the dam at the S end of Loch Turret and
take the track on the NE shore. From the head of the
loch climb the SW slopes of the hill to the broad dome
of the hill's summit and large cairn. Descend due W
from the summit to upper Glen Turret and follow the
track back to the dam.
Stalking Information: Glen Turret Estates.
Tel: 0764-652927.

5 Rannoch and Glen Lyon

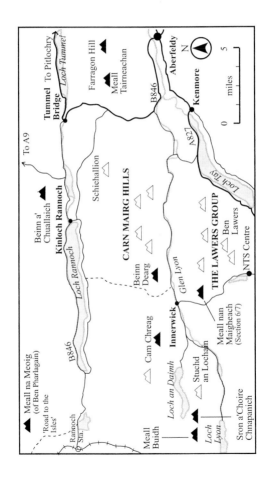

Suggested Base	Aberfeldy.
Accommodation	Hotels, guest houses and b&b at Fortingall, Kinloch Rannoch, Kenmore and Aberfeldy. Youth hostel at Killin. Camping/caravan sites at Kenmore, Kinloch Rannoch, Tummel Bridge and Aberfeldy.
Public Transport	Rail: London, Glasgow and Edinburgh to Inverness. Stations at Perth, Dunkeld and Pitlochry for ongoing buses. Rannoch Station on West Highland line for ongoing post bus. Buses: Perth and Pitlochry to Aberfeldy; Pitlochry to Kinloch Rannoch. Post Buses: Aberfeldy to Lubreoch in Glen Lyon; Kinloch Rannoch to Rannoch Station.

Mountain: Sron a'Choire Chnapanich, 2746ft/837m
　　　　　　Meall Buidhe, 2985ft/910m.
Map: OS Sheet 51: GR 456453, GR 427450.
Translation: nose of the lumpy corrie, yellow hill.
Pronunciation: *sron a corrie knapaneech, myowl boo-ee.*
Access Point: Loch Lyon Dam.

Sron a'Choire Chnapanich above Loch Daimh

Distance/ascent: 9mls/2700ft; 14km/823m.
Approx Time: 4-6 hours.
Route: Walk west along the path which runs along the N shore of Loch Lyon. After about half a mile leave the path and take a rising traverse line on the slopes of Meall Phubuill in a NW direction. Continue on this line until you reach the bealach between Creag Chaorrainn and the foot of Meall Buidhe's SE ridge. This bealach also splits the headwaters of the Eas nan Aighean and the Feith Thalain. Continue N, following an old fence, up the broad ridge and as it levels out bear W to cross another col. From here continue W to the summit of Meall Buidhe. Return to the bealach above the Feith Thalain and descend in a NE direction along the line of the burn for just over half a mile. Bear E to reach another col below the easy SW slopes of Sron a'Choire Chnapanich. Climb these slopes to the small summit cairn overlooking Loch an Daimh. Descend S from the summit, bearing slightly to the SSE as you descend to avoid the peat bogs at the head of the Allt Phubuill. Descend to Pubil and return to the dam along the road.
Stalking Information: Lochs Estate.
Tel: 08876-224.

Mountain: Cam Chreag, 2828ft/862m.
Map: OS Sheet 51: GR 536491.
Translation: crooked crag.
Pronunciation: *cam krayk.*
Access Point: Innerwick.
Distance/ascent: 7mls/2000ft; 11km/610m.
Approx Time: 3-5 hours.
Route: Leave the car park on the W side of the river in a NW direction and cross the Allt a'Choire Uidhre. Further W the track crosses the stream again and you should continue WNW to reach a hut which lies below the E face of Cam Chreag. Thread your way up through the crags of the E face to the broad summit shoulder and the summit cairn. Descend the same way.
Stalking Information: Meggernie Estate.
Tel: 08876-247.

Mountain: Beinn Dearg, 2723ft/830m.
Map: OS Sheet 51: GR 609497.
Translation: red hill.
Pronunciation: *byn jerrack.*
Access Point: Innerwick.
Distance/ascent: 6mls/2000ft; 10km/610m.
Approx Time: 3-5 hours.
Route: From Innerwick take the track up the E bank of
the river, continue through the forest and from above
the confluence of the Allt Ghallabhaich, (Allt Chalbhath
on the OS First Series map) and the Allt a'Choire Uidhre
climb the SW flank of Beinn Dearg. From the summit
descend W, then S then SE around the broad ridge of
Creag Ard. Descend to Innerwick W, then SW to avoid
the steepest slopes and the forestry. Beinn Dearg can be
combined with Cam Chreag by crossing the confluence
of the Allt Ghallabhaich and the Allt a'Choire Uidhre,
but in times of spate this can prove to be very difficult,
if not uncrossable.
Stalking Information: Meggernie Estate.
Tel: 08876-247.

Mountain: Farragon Hill, 2569ft/783m
           Meall Tairneachan, 2582ft/787m.
Map: OS Sheet 52: GR 841553, GR 807544.
Translation: Feargain's hill, (after St. Feargain, Abbot
of Iona), hill of thunder.
Pronunciation: *Fergan hill, myowl tairneech-an .*
Access Point: Blackhill on the B846.
Distance/ascent: 10mls/3000ft; 16km/914m.
Approx Time: 5-7 hours.
Route: Leave the B846 road at Blackhill and take the
forest road NW to Loch Derculich. Pass the loch and
continue to the high point of the road before turning
due W to climb Farragon Hill. Descend SW, taking care
to avoid the crags. Continue on the ridge in a WSW
direction for some distance before bearing due W to
cross a wet corrie. At point GR 827550 pick up another
track and follow it WSW to a barytes mine. Pass the
mine, continuing on the track to its highest point. From
there climb the N slopes of Meall Tairneachan to the

summit. To descend, either return the way you came over Farragon Hill, (14mls/3300ft; 23km/1006m) or return to the track to the N of the summit and continue along it NW through new forest plantations to the B846 north of Loch Kinardochy.
Stalking Information: Garrows Estate, Amulree, Dunkeld, Perthshire.
Tel: 0350-725216.

Mountain: Beinn a'Chuallaich, 2926ft/892m.
Map: OS Sheet 42: GR 684618.
Translation: hill of the herding.
Pronunciation: *byn a choo-aleech.*
Access Point: B847, GR 707616.
Distance/ascent: 4mls/1900ft; 6km/579m.
Approx Time: 3-5 hours.
Route: Leave the B847 and follow the stalker's path W which leads to a small bothy. Leave the track and climb across the slopes in a W direction to reach the burn which flows down from the corrie between Beinn a'Chuallaich and Meall nan Eun. Follow this burn in a NW direction into the corrie and climb steepening slopes onto the ridge N of the summit. Return S to the large summit cairn. You can either descend the way you came, or, if you can arrange transport back to the starting point continue W from the summit to reach a stalkers' path which runs S to Drumglas by Dunalastair Water. Even better is to continue W from the summit, cross this stalkers' path, bear SW and descend the slopes to the Allt Mor where another stalkers' path is picked up. This path takes you directly S to Kinloch Rannoch.
Stalking Information: Crossmount Estate.
Tel: 08822-305.

Mountain: Meall na Meoig (of Beinn Pharlagain) 2848ft/868m.
Map: OS Sheet 42: GR 448642.
Translation: hill of whey.
Pronunciation: *myowl na myaweek.*
Access Point: GR 445579, The Road to the Isles, B846 Rannoch Station road.

Distance/ascent: 9mls/2100ft; 14km/640m.
Approx Time: 5-7 hours.
Route: Take the Road to the Isles track from the N shore of Loch Eigheach. Follow the track as far as the footbridge over the Allt Eigheach, then bear NNE to climb the S slopes leading to Leacann nan Giomach. Continue N over the undulating ridge bearing NE to Pt 838m then NW to the large summit cairn of Meall na Meoig. Return the same way, or for a longer continuation taking in two Munros, continue N from Meall na Meoig to Sgor Gaibhre, WSW to Carn Dearg and S along the Sron Leachd a' Chaorainn, dropping down to pick up the Road to the Isles path again.
Stalking Information: Dunan Estate.
Tel: 08823-230.

6&7 The Killin Hills

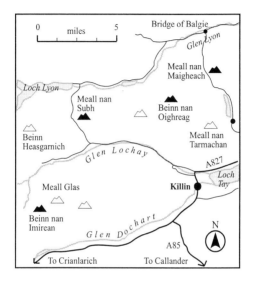

Suggested Base	Killin.
Accommodation	Hotels, guest houses and b&b in Killin, Kenmore, Lochearnhead, Fortingall and Aberfeldy. Youth hostel in Killin. Camping/caravan sites at Glendochart and Kenmore. Caravan site at Killin.
Public Transport	Rail: Glasgow to Stirling and Perth for ongoing buses. Also Glasgow to Crianlarich with on-going bus connections. Buses: Stirling to Killin, Perth to Aberfeldy for ongoing post buses. Post Buses: Aberfeldy to Killin and Crianlarich to Killin.

Mountain: Beinn nan Imirean, 2785ft/849m.
Map: OS Sheet 51: GR 419309.
Translation: hill of the ridge.
Pronunciation: *byn nan yeemaran.*
Access Point: A85, GR 448275.
Distance/ascent: 6mls/2300ft; 10km/701m.
Approx Time: 4-5 hours.
Route: Leave the A85 and follow the private road to Auchessan. A track continues up the E bank of the burn for some distance. When the track stops, continue to follow the burn, past the crags of Creag nan Uan to the foot of Beinn nan Imirean's SE ridge, Meall Garbh. Climb this ridge to the summit of Beinn nan Imirean. Descend the same route.
Stalking Information: Invermearan Estate.
Tel: 08876-244.

Mountain: Meall nan Subh, 2645ft/806m.
Map: OS Sheet 51: GR 461397.
Translation: hill of the raspberry.
Pronunciation: *myowl nan soo.*
Access Point: Gate on the Lairig nan Lunn road, GR 452386.
Distance/ascent: 2mls/1000ft; 3km/305m.
Approx Time: 2 hours.
Route: The gate near the summit of the Lairig nan Lunn road is sometimes locked so drive as far as this gate from either the north or the south. Park at the gate and make your way to the highest point of the road, marked by a cairn. From the cairn ascend the slopes in a NE direction to the summit to climb what is probably the easiest of all the Corbetts!
Stalking Information: Cashlie Estate.
Tel: 08876-237.

Mountain: Beinn nan Oighreag, 2982ft/909m
                Meall nam Maigheach, (Meall Luaidhe)
                2558ft/780m.
Map: OS Sheet 51: GR 543414, GR 586436.
Translation: cloudberry hill, hill of the hare.

Pronunciation: *byn nan oe-eerak, myowl nam my-eech.*
Access Point: Lochan na Lairige road, GR 582417.
Distance/ascent: 8mls/2750ft; 13km/838m.
Approx Time: 5-7 hours.
Route: Leave the Lochan na Lairige road at the small hut in a W direction, crossing the N ridge of Beinn nan Eachan into the boggy Lairig Breisleich. From the Lairig climb due W to the summit of Beinn nan Oighreag. Return to the hut by the Lochan na Lairige road. (A more satisfactory approach to this hill is by way of the Lairig Breisleich from the power station in Glen Lochay in the S.) To climb Meall nam Maigheach, (on the first series OS maps this hill is shown as Meall Luaidhe.) follow the road N from the hut for just over half a mile to where a burn flows down from Meall nan Eun. Leave the road here and climb the hill in a NNE direction all the way to the summit. There may be a temptation to descend the obvious ridge to Meall nan Eun and then SW to the road but avoid this — there are many peat hags around this area which makes miserable walking. Descend the way of ascent.
Stalking Information: Meggernie Estate.
Tel: 08876-247.

8, 9&10 Etive and Glencoe

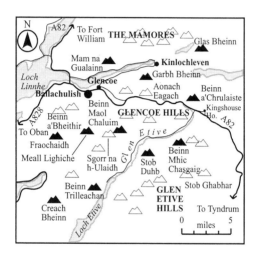

Suggested Base	Glencoe or Kingshouse.
Accommodation	Hotels, guest houses and b&b in Glencoe, Carnoch, Kinlochleven, Onich and Ballachulish. Hotel and bunkhouse at Kingshouse. Youth hostel in Glencoe. Camping and caravan sites in Glencoe and Onich. Private bunkhouses at Clachaig Inn, Leacantium, Glencoe and at Kingshouse Hotel.
Public Transport	Rail: Glasgow to Fort William. Nearest station at Fort William or Bridge of Orchy for connecting buses. Buses: Glasgow to Fort William for Kingshouse, Glencoe and Ballachulish. Oban to Fort William for Ballachulish.

■■■■■■■■■■■■■■■■■

Mountain: Creach Bheinn, 2657ft/810m.
Map: OS Sheet 50: GR 024422.
Translation: windswept hill.
Pronunciation: kreych ven.
Access Point: A828, GR 007451.
Distance/ascent: 9mls/2800ft; 14km/853m.
Approx Time: 5-7 hours.
Route: Leave the road N of Druimavuic House where a gate gives access to a path through some woodland. Once clear of the house this path follows the N bank of the Allt Buidhe to the bealach between the Munro Beinn Sgulaird and Creach Bheinn. From the bealach follow the well defined NE ridge of Creach Bheinn over Creag na Cathaig then steeply due W to the NE top of Creach Bheinn. A short descent to the SW and a short climb lead to the large cairn.
Stalking Information: Ardchattan Estate.
Tel: 063171-274.

■■■■■■■■■■■■■■■■■

Mountain: Beinn Trilleachan, 2752ft/839m.
Map: OS Sheet 50: GR 086439.
Translation: hill of the sandpipers.
Pronunciation: byn tryl-yach-an.
Access Point: Gualachulain, Glen Etive.
Distance/ascent: 7mls/3000ft; 11km/914m.
Approx Time: 5-7 hours.
Route: About 300m north of the pier at the head of Loch Etive a fairly indistinct path starts at the edge of the forest. Follow this path onto the NE ridge of Beinn Trilleachan. Follow this ridge in a SW direction, cross the first top, Meall nan Gobhar, and continue along the increasingly rocky crest to the second top which is marked by a cairn which sits in an exposed position above the sweep of the Etive Slabs. Descend slightly, then climb gently SW to the summit.
Stalking Information: Forestry Commission.
Tel: 0631-66155.

■■■■■■■■■■■■■■■■■

Mountain: Stob Dubh, 2897ft/883m.
Map: OS Sheet 50: GR 166488.

Stob Dubh from the head of Loch Etive

Translation: black peak.
Pronunciation: *stop doo.*
Access Point: Glen Etive road, GR 137468.
Distance/ascent: 7mls/3200ft; 11km/975m.
Approx Time: 4-6 hours.
Route: Leave the road and follow the private track which crosses the river to Coileitir. Once over the bridge however, turn left and follow the track for just over half a mile to the Allt Ceitlein. Cross the burn by the footbridge and climb the long and steep SW ridge of Stob Dubh, avoiding the odd crag and outcrop on the right. As the summit is reached the angle of the gradient eases off. Rather than descend the way you came, drop down steeply in an ESE direction before the ridge curls round to the NE and leads to the first of two summits of Beinn Ceitlin, which is the highest point. Descend in a SE direction over steep and rough ground. After several hundred feet bear S to the headwaters of the Allt Ceitlin. Follow the burn back to the bridge.
Stalking Information: National Trust for Scotland.
Tel: 08552-311/307.

Mountain: Beinn Mhic Chasgaig, 2835ft/864m.
Map: OS Sheets 41 and 50: GR 221502.
Translation: McCasgaig's hill.
Pronunciation: *byn mic casgaig.*

Access Point: Glen Etive road at Alltchaorunn, GR 198513.

Distance/ascent: 4½mls/2500ft; 7km/762m.

Approx Time: 4-6 hours.

Route: Cross the bridge over the River Etive. If the gate on the bridge is locked you may have to ford the river, but bear in mind that the River Etive is fordable only in good weather and most certainly not after times of heavy or prolonged rain. On the far side of the bridge a track runs SW to Alltchaorunn, beyond which a track follows the line of the Allt a'Chaorainn. At any point after the first quarter mile of track you can take to the hill and the steep W ridge. The crags higher up the ridge can easily be avoided. Follow the ridge to the broad summit plateau with the cairn at the N end.

The ascent of Beinn Mhic Chasgaig is often combined with a traverse of the Munros Clachlet and Creise.

Stalking Information: National Trust for Scotland.

Tel: 08552-311/307.

Mountain: Beinn a'Chrulaiste, 2811ft/857m.

Map: OS Sheet 41: GR 246567.

Translation: rocky hill.

Pronunciation: *byn a kroo-las-tay*.

Access Point: Altnafeadh, GR 221563.

Distance/ascent: Complete traverse; 6mls/2000ft; 10km/610m.

Approx Time: 4-6 hours.

Route: Follow the path of the Devil's Staircase for a quarter of a mile or so then take the W ridge of the hill to Stob Beinn a'Chrulaiste. Most of the crags lie on the S side of this ridge. From the Stob bear NE then E to follow the ridge to the broad summit and trig point.

An alternative descent, making a complete traverse of the hill, is to drop off the summit in a SE direction, (there are more rocky outcrops and crags hereabouts than the map suggests) towards the line of the Allt a'Bhalaich. Follow the burn down to Kingshouse and follow the route of the West Highland Way back to Altnafeadh.

Stalking Information: Black Corries Estate.

Tel: 08556-272.

Beinn a'Chrulaiste from Blackrock Cottage

Mountain: Beinn Maol Chaluim, 2975ft/907m.
Map: OS Sheet 41 and 50: GR135526.
Translation: Calum's bare hill.
Pronunciation: *byn moel hallum.*
Access Point: Glen Etive road, GR 149496.
Distance/ascent: 5mls/2600ft; 8km/792m.
Approx Time: 4-6 hours.
Route: Leave the road and climb steep grassy slopes beside the forestry fence. Pass some rocky outcrops and reach the S ridge of Beinn Maol Chaluim. Continue northwards on the ridge, avoiding some awkward crags on their right. Pass the southern tops and continue NW on the ridge to the summit cairn. Return the same way. This Corbett can be linked with the Munro Bidean nam Bian by descending N to the head of Gleann Fhaolain and climbing Bidean by its steep SW aspect. Return to the starting point by following the ridge over Stob Coire Sgreamhach.
Stalking Information: Glen Etive Estate.
Tel: 08556-277 or 08384-283.

Mountain: Meall Ligiche, 2533ft/772m.
Map: OS Sheet 41: GR 095529.
Translation: doctor's hill.
Pronunciation: *myowl lie-eecha.*

Access Point: A82, small lay-by at GR 118565.
Distance/ascent: 6mls/2500ft; 10km/762m.
Approx Time: 5-7 hours.
Route: Cross the road and follow the track which runs to Gleann-leac-na-muidhe. Continue following the track through the farm and on for a further one and half miles to an obvious stream junction where the track ends. Cross the Allt na Muidhe and ascend the rough NE slopes of Creag Bhan, threading your way through some obvious crags. Bear S and follow the terraced ridge to the summit of Creag Bhan. From here the ridge twists sharply W where a line of old fence posts lead over undulating ground to the summit cairn which sits at the W end of the ridge. Either descend by the same route, or drop down the slopes SSE of Creag Bhan and the headwaters of the Allt na Muidhe. Follow the faint path on the E bank of the burn back to Gleann-leac-na-muidhe.

Meall Ligiche can be linked to the Munro, Sgor na h-Ulaidh by the bealach SSE of Creag Bhan.
Stalking Information: Forestry Commission.
Tel: 0631-66155.

Mountain: Fraochaidh, 2833ft/863m.
Map: OS Sheet 41: GR 029517.
Translation: heathery hill.
Pronunciation: *free-achy.*
Access Point: Ballachulish, GR 081579.
Distance/ascent: 12mls/3300ft; 19km/1006m.
Approx Time: 6-8 hours.
Route: Fraochaidh is well surrounded by forestry plantations making access, in most cases, difficult. The following route is one of a number of possibilities, but has the advantage of being free of conifers. Leave the minor road which runs south from East Laroch in Ballachulish. Continue on this road as it becomes a track and then a footpath. After a couple of miles, at a cairn, another path (the right of way to Glen Creran) drops off to the left to cross the River Laroch. Follow this faint path up steep grassy slopes to the forestry fence, turn right along the forestry fence for quarter of a mile or so before leaving it to ascend the first top of the long curved ridge which leads to Fraochaidh. Follow this

ridge SSW, passing a small lochan and continue to the next top at 718m. The ridge now becomes narrower and rockier and curves SW then WNW for the final pull up to the level summit and the cairn. Avoid the conifers by returning the same way.
Stalking Information: Forestry Commission.
Tel: 0631-66155.

Mountain: Garbh Bheinn, 2844ft/867m.
Map: OS Sheet 41: GR 169601.
Translation: rough hill.
Pronunciation: garav-vyn.
Access Point: Caolasnacon, B863.
Distance/ascent: 4mls/2800ft; 6km/853m.
Approx Time: 3-5 hours.
Route: Leave the small lay-by near the bridge over the Allt Gleann a'Chaolais. On the Kinlochleven side of the bridge leave the road and follow the footpath beside the river for a short distance before heading due E onto the W ridge of Garbh Bheinn. Follow the faint path between rocky outcrops up the ridge, over a number of false summits to the double cairned top. The first is the highest. Descend either the same way, or continue over the mountain in a complete traverse, down the NE ridge to Kinlochleven, returning to Caolasnacon by the road.
Stalking Information: National Trust for Scotland.
Tel: 08552-311/307.

Mountain: Mam na Gualainn, 2611ft/796m.
Map: OS Sheet 41: GR 115625.
Translation: pass of the shoulder.
Pronunciation: mam na goo-aleen.
Access Point: Callert, B863, GR 097605.
Distance/ascent: 5mls/2500ft; 8km/762m.
Approx Time: 4-6 hours.
Route: Just east of Callert House there is a right of way which runs over the W shoulder of Mam na Gualainn to Lairigmor. Follow this route for just over a mile until you are adjacent to the high point of the adjoining forestry plantation. Leave the path here and follow the

WSW ridge of Mam na Gualainn to the summit. An alternative descent continues E to Beinn na Caillich and then down to the West Highland Way which leads to Mamore Lodge and Kinlochleven. Either return to the start by road, or use two cars.
Stalking Information: British Alcan.
Tel: 0397-2433.

Mountain: Glas Bheinn, 2597ft/792m.
Map: OS Sheet 41: GR 259641.
Translation: grey hill.
Pronunciation: glash vyn.
Access Point: Grey Mare Waterfall car park, Kinlochleven.
Distance/ascent: 10mls/2600ft; 16km/792m.
Approx Time: 5-8 hours.
Route: Leave the car park and follow the path through the woods and out onto the hillside. Continue as far as the track which links Loch Eilde Mor and Mamore Lodge. Walk E on this track for a short distance before taking another path which goes round the E end of the loch to a dam. From the dam another path leads ENE then ESE to cross the Meall na Cruaidhe shoulder of Glas Bheinn. As the path crosses this shoulder leave it and follow the broad SW ridge of Glas Bheinn to the summit. Return the same way. A much longer alternative descent follows the NNE ridge of the mountain to the Abhainn Rath, then follows the track from Luibelt back along the N shore of Loch Eilde Mor.
Stalking Information: British Alcan.
Tel: 0397-2433.

11,12&13 Loch Trieg and Loch Ossian

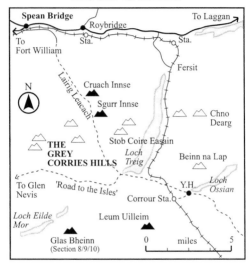

Suggested Base Accommodation	Fersit, near Tulloch, Spean Bridge. Private hostel at Fersit. Hotels, guest houses and b&b at Spean Bridge and Roybridge.
Public Transport	Rail: West Highland Line Glasgow to Fort William stopping at Corrour, Tulloch and Roybridge. Buses: Fort William to Aviemore stopping at Tulloch.

Mountain: Leum Uilleim, 2972ft/906m.
Map: OS Sheet 41: GR 331641.
Translation: William's leap.
Pronunciation: lie-aim oolyam.
Access Point: Corrour Station, West Highland Line.
Distance/ascent: 6mls/2000ft; 10km/610m.

Approx Time: 4-6 hours.
Route: Leave the station and head W along the track until it ends. Continue in a W direction and climb the slopes to reach the NE ridge of Beinn a'Bhric. Follow the ridge to the summit, descend steep slopes to the E and from the col climb the slopes to the summit of Leum Uilleim. Descend by following the rocky NE ridge (Sron an Lagain Ghairbh) down to some boggy flats and back to the station.
Stalking Information: British Alcan.
Tel: 0397-2433.

Mountain: Cruach Innse, 2812ft/857m
          Sgurr Innse, 2654ft/809m.
Map: OS Sheet 41: GR 280763, GR 290748.
Translation: hill of the meadow, peak of the meadow.
Pronunciation: *krooach eensha, skoor eensha.*
Access Point: GR 256788, Lairig Leacach. (Take public road from Spean Bridge to Corriechoille, then the right of way to Rannoch. You can drive as far as the old tramway at the above grid reference.).
Distance/ascent: 8mls/3200ft; 13kms/975m.
Approx Time: 6-8 hours.
Route: Drive as far as the old tramway on the Lairig Leacach, just short of the forestry plantation. Follow the track through the plantation, and over the Allt Leachdach. A couple of hundred metres past the bridge take to the hillside, following heathery slopes to the NW ridge of Cruach Innse. Continue up this broad ridge to the flat stony summit. Descend in a SE direction down fairly easy slopes and as the slopes become steeper bear S avoiding the crags. From the broad col climb SE to below the rocky crest of Sgurr Innse. A large area of boulder scree gives access to a leftward slanting shelf, where a faint path climbs to the N shoulder of the hill and a straightforward climb to the summit. Take care on the descent as a path appears to lead W down a scree filled gully. This gully is very loose and ends abruptly above a 20ft crag. Descend the way of ascent, back to the col where you can drop down easy slopes into the Lairig Leacach.
Stalking Information: British Alcan.
Tel: 0397-2433.

14&15 Loch Ericht and Drumochter

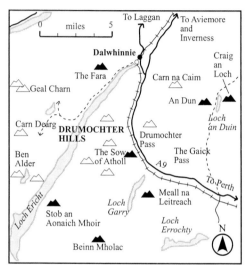

Suggested Base	Blair Atholl.
Accommodation	Hotels, guest houses and b&b at Pitlochry, Blair Atholl, Dalwhinnie and Newtonmore and Kingussie. Youth hostels at Kingussie and Pitlochry. Camping and caravan sites at Blair Atholl and Glen Truim, Newtonmore.
Public Transport	Rail: Glasgow and Edinburgh to Inverness. stops at Pitlochry, Blair Atholl, Dalwhinnie and Kingussie. Buses: London, Glasgow and Edinburgh to Perth and Inverness for Blair Atholl, Dalwhinnie, Newtonmore and Kingussie.

Mountain: Stob an Aonaich Mhoir, 2805ft/855m
                   Beinn Mholach, 2759ft/841m.
Map: OS Sheet 42: GR 537694, GR 587655.
Translation: peak of the big crest, shaggy mountain.
Pronunciation: stob an oenach vore, byn voe-lach.
Access Point: Bridge of Ericht, Loch Rannoch.
Distance/ascent: 1. Stob an Aonaich Mhoir from the
Bridge of Ericht road — 16 mls/2100ft; 26km/640m.
2. Beinn Mholach from Annat — 11mls/2100ft;
18km/640m. 3. Beinn Mholach from Dalnaspidal —
12mls/1500ft; 19km/457m.
Approx Time: 1. 7-9 hours (by foot); 2. 6-8 hours;
3. 6-8 hours.
Route: Take the tarmac road which runs N from Bridge
of Ericht on the N shore of Loch Rannoch. A bicycle
would be useful for this 7 mile stretch of road which
runs to its highest point just below the E slopes of Stob
an Aonaich Mhoir. From this point, climb these E slopes
to the summit and return back to the road again. It is
possible to reach Beinn Mholach from this point also
by climbing the NW slopes of Glas Mheall Mor, descending S to the wide col below Beinn Bhoidheach
and then crossing another broad col in an E direction to
reach Beinn Mholach. This is a high and exposed walk
over a lot of peaty ground. Possibly better to approach
Beinn Mholach from Annat on the N shore of Loch
Rannoch. Follow the right of way which runs to Loch
Garry and climb the hill by its SE slopes. A more direct
route begins at the S end of Loch Garry (access by
Dalnaspidal Lodge on the A9, Perth to Inverness road)
and climbs the hill by its NE ridge.
Stalking Information: Stob an Aonaich Mhoir –
Talladh-a-Bheithe Estate; tel: 0887-20496. Beinn
Mholach, from Annat – Talladh-a-Bheithe Estate; tel:
0887-20496. From Dalnaspidal – Dalnaspidal Estate;
tel: 079683-204.

Mountain: Meall na Leitreach, 2544ft/775m
          The Sow of Atholl, 2634ft/803m.
Map: OS Sheet 42: GR 639703, GR 6257422.
Translation: hill of slopes. The Sow of Atholl was origi-
nally Meall an Dobhrachan, hill of the watercress.
Pronunciation: myowl na lie-ay-troch.
Access Point: Dalnaspidal, A9, Perth to Inverness road.
Distance/ascent: 7mls/2600ft; 11kms/792m.
Approx Time: 4-6 hours.
Route: Leave Dalnaspidal and head towards Loch
Garry. Use the various footbridges to cross the rivers.
Once across the River Garry head SSE up heathery
slopes to a wide summit plateau, very peaty in places.
Head SSW across this plateau, avoiding the peat hags
as much as possible. The summit cairn is in the middle
of a wide dome. Return the same way to the head of
Loch Garry and climb The Sow of Atholl by its broad
and heathery SE ridge. Return the same way.
Stalking Information: Dalnaspidal Estate.
Tel: 079683-204.

Mountain: An Dun, 2713ft/827m
          Creag an Loch, 2890ft/881m.
Map: OS Sheet 42: GR 716802, GR 735807.
Translation: the fort, cliff of the loch.
Pronunciation: an doon, krayk an loch.
Access Point: Dalnacardoch, A9, Perth to Inverness
road.
Distance/ascent: 18mls/3000ft; 29km/914m.
Approx Time: 8-10 hours.
Route: A bulldozed track runs N from the A9 from
Dalnacardoch Lodge all the way to beyond
Sronphadruig Lodge at the southern end of Loch an
Duin. This track, which is almost 6 miles in length, is
easily negotiated by bicycle. Beyond Sronphadruig
Lodge the bulldozed track terminates at a small dam.
From the dam, climb the steep heather slopes of An
Dun in a N direction. It's a short, but steep haul to the
summit plateau and the cairn. Return the same way,
avoiding the precipitous E facing slopes, to the track.
Return towards the Lodge again but before you reach

it, at the N end of the plantation, head SE for the obvious col between Creag an Loch and the hill marked 621m. From the col, turn N along the ridge and follow it until it becomes part of a wide, expansive summit plateau. The summit cairn is the first of two at its N end. This hill is referred to in the SMC Corbett's guide as Maol Creag an Loch, although it is known locally simply as Creag an Loch. The OS name the N ridge as A'Chaoirnich, just to complicate matters. Return to Sronphadruig Lodge and the long walk, or cycle, to Dalnacardoch.

Stalking Information: Dalnacardoch Estate.
Tel: 0764-553.

Mountain: The Fara, 2989ft/911m.
Map: OS Sheet 42: GR 598844.
Translation: possibly from faradh, ladder.
Pronunciation: fara.
Access Point: Lay-by on A889 north of Dalwhinnie, GR 637858.
Distance/ascent: 6mls/1800ft; 10km/549m.
Approx Time: 3-5 hours.
Route: Take the new forest track which leads SW onto the E facing slopes of The Fara. This wide track eventually narrows and as it steadily climbs it gradually becomes no more than a forestry furrow. Follow it to its end, climb the fence and take the steeper heathery slopes in a NW direction, eventually following an old fence and stone dyke to the huge summit cairn. It's worthwhile following the ridge S for about a mile for the extensive views down the length of Loch Ericht to Rannoch Moor and beyond. Descend by the NW ridge to the Allt an t-Sluic which can be followed back to the start.

Stalking Information: Ben Alder Estate.
Tel: 05282-224/230

16 Pitlochry, Tarf and Tilt

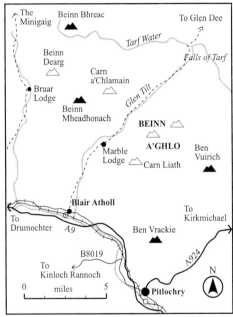

Suggested Base	Pitlochry or Blair Atholl.
Accommodation	Hotels, guest houses, b&b in Pitlochry, Killicrankie and Blair Atholl. Youth hostel in Pitlochry. Camping & caravan sites in Pitlochry and Blair Atholl.
Public Transport	Rail: Glasgow and Edinburgh to Inverness, stopping at Blair Atholl and Pitlochry. Buses: Glasgow and Edinburgh to Inverness. Stops at Pitlochry and Blair Atholl.

Ben Vrackie above Pitlochry

Mountain: Ben Vrackie, 2759ft/841m.
Map: OS Sheets 43 and 52: GR 951632.
Translation: speckled hill.
Pronunciation: *byn vraackee.*
Access Point: Car park at Moulin, A924 (down a lane behind the Moulin Inn).
Distance/ascent: 5mls/2000ft; 8km/610m.
Approx Time: 3-5 hours.
Route: Leave the car park, and follow the signposted path through mixed woodland to a gate which gives access to moorland. Continue on the footpath in a N direction to the obvious col between Creag Bhreac and Meall na h-Aodainn Moire. Continue over the shallow col and cross the dam at the E end of Loch a'Choire. From here climb the eroded path which climbs the steep slopes just E of Ben Vrackie's SW crags. Reach the summit ridge, bearing left for the final few feet to the summit and a direction indicator. Return the same way.
 Stalking Information: Baledmund Estate.
Tel: 0796-2721.

Mountain: Ben Vuirich, 2962ft/903m.
Map: OS Sheet 43: GR 997700.
Translation: hill of roaring.
Pronunciation: *byn voo-rich.*
Access Point: Loch Moraig, above Blair Atholl, GR 907672.

Distance/ascent: 13mls/2300ft; 21km/701m.
Approx Time: 6-8 hours.
Route: Take the estate road E from Loch Moraig skirting the S slopes of Carn Liath. Continue on this track as far as the footbridge over the Allt Coire Lagain. Cross the river and turn left before the old building at Shinigaig. Keep following the track across the S slopes of Meall Breac to its end, where the going becomes peaty and fairly rough. Head E climbing the slopes of Creag nan Gobhar to Ben Vuirich's S ridge. Follow the ridge to the summit. Return via Vuirich's W slopes to Loch Valigan and down by the Allt Loch Valigan to a footpath which returns S to Shinigaig. Follow the estate road back to Loch Moraig.
Stalking Information: Lude Estate.
Tel: 079681-240.

Mountain: Beinn Mheadhonach, 2956ft/901m.
Map: OS Sheet 43: GR 880758.
Translation: middle hill.
Pronunciation: *byn vee-onach.*
Access Point: Gilbert's bridge, Glen Tilt GR 881701.
Distance/ascent: 8mls/2400ft; 13km/732m.
Approx Time: 4-6 hours.
Route: Either follow the footpath from Middlebridge near Blair Atholl or drive up to Gilbert's Bridge. (Permit costs £5 from Blair Atholl Estate Factor's Office — phone number below) From the bridge cross to the W bank of the river and follow the forestry road. After a short distance a footpath leaves the forestry road and threads its way through the trees closer to the river's W bank. Follow this to the small gorge of the Allt Mhairc. Cross the burn by the bridge and continue on the path, now climbing in a NNW. Higher up, beyond its junction with the Allt Diridh, another bridge crosses the Allt Mhairc. Cross this and climbing in a NW direction ascend the heathery slopes to reach the mountain's S ridge. Pass a large cairn on the E side of the ridge and continue to the narrow summit plateau. The cairn sits at the N end, beyond several other cairns which you'll pass en route.
Stalking Information: Atholl Estate.
Tel: 079681-355.

Mountain: Beinn Bhreac, 2992ft/912m.
Map: OS Sheet 43: GR 868821.
Translation: speckled hill.
Pronunciation: *byn vrechk.*
Access Point: Calvine, A9. GR 804659.
Distance/ascent: From Bruar Lodge — 8mls/1600ft; 13km/488m.
Approx Time: 4-6 hours.
Route: Take the estate road which runs for 8mls/13km to Bruar Lodge. A bicycle would be useful. Continue on the track past the lodge for about half a mile then take the stalker's path which follows the N bank of the Allt Beinn Losgarnaich. Continue on boggy ground over the watershed between Beinn Losgarnaich and Beinn Dearg, and head NE to another boggy watershed between the headwaters of the Tarf Water and the Allt a' Chuil. Continue NE up the uniform slopes of Beinn Bhreac to the summit. Return the same way.
Stalking Information: Atholl Estate.
Tel: 079681-355.

17&18 Cairnwell, Glenshee and Lochnagar

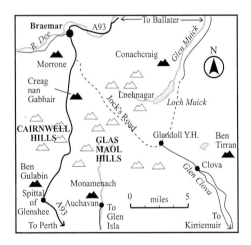

Suggested Base	Braemar.
Accommodation	Hotels, guest houses and b&b in Braemar, Ballater, Glenshee, Blairgowrie. Youth hostels at Braemar, Ballater. Camping and caravan sites at Braemar, Ballater and Blairgowrie.
Public Transport	Rail: London, Glasgow and Edinburgh to Dundee and Aberdeen. Buses: Aberdeen to Braemar and Ballater. Dundee to Kirriemuir and Blairgowrie for onward post bus service. Post Buses: Blairgowrie to Spittal of Glenshee.

Mountain: Ben Gulabin, 2645ft/806m.
Map: OS Sheet 43: GR 101722.
Translation: hill of the beaked bird.
Pronunciation: byn goolavyn.
Access Point: Lay-by on A93 N of Spittal of Glenshee,
GR 114714.
Distance/ascent: 3mls/1500ft; 5km/457m.
Approx Time: 2-3 hours.
Route: From the lay-by a gate gives access to a track
which climbs the E slopes of Gulabin in a N direction.
Continue on this track to the col between Gulabin and
Creagan Bheithe. From the old building at the end of
the track climb Ben Gulabin in a WSW direction to the
summit. An alternative descent follows the S ridge back
to Spittal of Glenshee.
Stalking Information: Invercauld Estate.
Tel: 03383-224.

Mountain: Monamenach, 2648ft/807m.
Map: OS Sheet 43: GR 176707.
Translation: middle hill.
Pronunciation: mona-vee-onach.
Access Point: Auchavan, Glen Isla, GR 191697.
Distance/ascent: 2½ mls/1500ft; 4km/457m.
Approx Time: 2-3 hours.
Route: From the end of the public road at Auchavan a
path runs NW to meet a burn flowing down from a high
col. Follow the path to its end, them strike NW up steep
slopes to the summit. An alternative descent is by the N
ridge to Tulchan Lodge, then return to Auchavan by the
track beside the River Isla.
Stalking Information: Tulchan Estate.
Tel: 057582-264.

Mountain: Creag nan Gabhar, 2736ft/834m.
Map: OS Sheet 43: GR 154841.
Translation: hill of the goats.
Pronunciation: krayk nan gower.
Access Point: A93, GR 140835.
Distance/ascent: 2½mls/1400ft; 4km/427m.
Approx Time: 2-3 hours.

Route: Park near the AA telephone box on the A93 and take the footpath which runs E towards the Bealach Buidhe between Creag nan Gabhar and Creag an t-Sean-ruigh. Continue on the path up the steep sided glen and after half a mile cross the stream to its N bank and ascend the S slopes of Creag nan Gabhar avoiding the scree slopes to the west. You can either return the same way, or continue N over Sron nan Gabhar and Sron Dubh, descending the stalkers path E into Glen Callater, returning to the starting point by the road.
Stalking Information: Invercauld Estate.
Tel: 03383-267.

Mountain: Morrone, 2819ft/859m.
Map: OS Sheet 43: GR 132886.
Translation: the big nose.
Pronunciation: *mor-own.*
Access Point: Braemar.
Distance/ascent: 1½mls/1400ft; 2.4km/427m.
*Approx Time:*1½ to 2hours.
Route: Starting point is a car park at the top of Chapel Brae in Braemar. A private road runs S to a direction indicator. Leave the road and take a track which runs to the left, leaving it almost immediately to follow a path which runs S around a knoll. Follow this path all the way to the summit. An alternative descent continues SW to a Landrover track which drops down to Glen Clunie opposite Auchallater farm.
Stalking Information: No restrictions.

Mountain: Conachcraig, 2838ft/865m.
Map: OS Sheet 44: GR 280865.
Translation: jumble of rocks.
Pronunciation: *konu-krayk.*
Access Point: Spittal of Glen Muick car park, GR 308851.
Distance/ascent: 5mls/1500ft; 8km/457m.
Approx Time: 3-4 hours.
Route: Leave the car park and follow the track which eventually runs to Allt-na-giubsaich. Take the Lochnagar path through the pines and once clear of the trees take to the open hillside in a NW direction.

Follow a broad spur to the col between Pt 865m and the summit. At this col turn right for the short rise to the summit. Return the same way or follow the ridge in a SW direction, past Pt 865m and down to the Lochnagar path, returning to Allt-na-giubsaich.
Stalking Information: Balmoral Estate.
Tel: 03384-334.

Mountain: Mount Battack, 2554ft/778m.
Map: OS Sheet 44: GR 549845.
Translation: Possibly anglicised from badag, chump.
Pronunciation: *mount baat-ack.*
Access Point: Glen Esk, GR 541791.
Distance/ascent: 9mls/2000ft; 14km/610m.
Approx Time: 4-6 hours.
Route: Start from Millden Lodge and follow the track N beside the Water of Turret. After a few hundred yards cross by a footbridge to the W bank and follow the track N to another crossing of the burn. Stay on the W bank and climb away from the burn in a NW direction, still following the stalker's track. Continue following the track till it ends high on the slopes of Mount Battack's broad SW ridge. Continue in a N direction to the W summit at Pt 717m, then follow the ridge in a ENE direction to the main summit. Return S by Hill of Slaughs and Hill of Turret.
Stalking Information: Glen Tanar Estate.
Tel: 0339-2393.

Mountain: Ben Tirran, 2941ft/896m.
Map: OS Sheet 44: GR 374746.
Translation: unknown.
Pronunciation: *ben turran.*
Access Point: Glen Clova, GR 353715.
Distance/ascent: 6mls/2200ft; 10km/670m.
Approx Time: 4-6 hours.
Route: Leave Wheen in Glen Clova and follow a track N up the side of a forestry plantation. At the top of the plantation join with another path at a burn and follow it N, eventually climbing the steep slopes of Ben Tirran's W ridge above Loch Wharral. From the top of the ridge cross the open plateau in a NE direction to the trig point

summit. Return either the same way or take an alternative route via Green Hill and Loch Brandy, descending
into Clova, about 1½mls/2.4km from your starting point.
Stalking Information: Airlie Estate.
Tel: 05755-230.

19 Southern Cairngorms

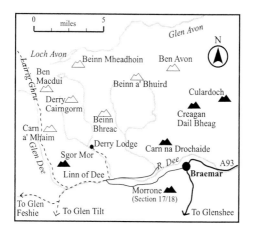

Suggested Base	Kingussie and Braemar.
Accommodation	Hotels, guest houses and b&b at Kingussie, Newtonmore and at Braemar. Youth hostels at Kingussie and Braemar. Private hostels in Kincraig and Newtonmore. Camp sites at Newtonmore and Braemar.
Public Transport	Rail: London, Glasgow and Edinburgh to Inverness, stations at Kingussie and Aviemore. London, Glasgow and Edinburgh to Aberdeen for onward bus service to Braemar. Buses: London, Glasgow and Edinburgh via Perth to Inverness for Kingussie and Aviemore. London, Edinburgh, Glasgow and Inverness to Aberdeen for onward bus service to Braemar.

Mountain: Meallach Mhor, 2522ft/769m.
Map: OS Sheet 35: GR 777909.
Translation: big hump.
Pronunciation: *myowlach vore.*
Access Point: Bhran Cottage, Glen Tromie, GR 752914.
Distance/ascent: From Bhran Cottage, 2½mls/1700ft;
4km/518m.
Approx Time: 1-2 hours.
Route: As the road up Glen Tromie is private and closed
to cars you'll have to either walk or cycle the 6mls/
11km up the glen to Bhran Cottage. Leave the tarred
road about a quarter of a mile beyond Bhran Cottage
and climb heathery slopes to the E of the Alltan Tulaich.
After a short initial climb veer ESE to gain the broad
W ridge. Follow this ridge directly to the stony sum-
mit. Return the same way.
Stalking Information: Glenfeshie Estate.
Tel: 05402-453.

Mountain: Leathad an Taobhain, 2991ft/912m
            Carn Dearg Mor, 2813ft/857m.
Map: OS Sheet 43: GR 822858, GR 824912.
Translation: slope of the rafters, big red cairn.
Pronunciation: *lye-at an tay-vin, kaarn jerrag mor.*
Access Point: Tolvah in Glen Feshie, GR 842997.
Distance/ascent: From Lochan an t-Sluic, 9mls/2700ft;
15km/823m.
Approx Time: 5-7 hours.
Route: Park at Tolvah in Glen Feshie, just before the
locked gate. You can either walk or cycle the 7mls/12km
up Glen Feshie, past the lodge to Lochan an t-Sluic.
From the lochan continue SW to a fork in the tracks.
Take the left fork and follow the bulldozed track to the
summit of Meall an Uillt Chreagaich. It is possible to
cycle this track on a mountain bike! At the end of the
track follow the narrow footpath which drops down to
an old ruin in a narrow col below, cross the stream and
climb the slopes in a S direction to the summit plateau
and trig point of Leathad an Taobhain. Return to the
col, climb back to the summit of Meall an Uillt
Chreagaich and return to the fork in the tracks before

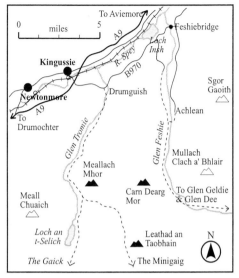

Lochan an t-Sluic. This time take the fork which turns W, then N and as the track veers steeply W again leave it and climb heathery slopes in a NNE direction to the summit of Carn Dearg Mor. Return to the fork in the tracks, then by tracks and road to Glen Feshie.
Stalking Information: Glenfeshie Estate.
Tel: 05402-453.

███████████████████

Mountain: Sgor Mor, 2667ft/813m.
Map: OS Sheet 43: GR 006914.
Translation: big peak.
Pronunciation: *skoor mor*.
Access Point: Car Park at Linn of Dee, GR 063897.
Distance/ascent: 10mls/1700ft; 16km/518m.
Approx Time: 4-6 hours.
Route: From the car park follow the track W alongside the River Dee, passing White Bridge and the Chest of Dee. About a mile beyond White Bridge, as the track turns up Glen Dee, take to the hillside at a double stream

junction and climb the broad S ridge of Sgor Mor which becomes increasingly stony, then slabby, as you approach the summit. From the summit, follow the broad whale-backed ridge in an ENE direction to the trig point on Sgor Dubh before dropping down the SE spur and over Carn an'lc Duibhe to the track which leads to Linn of Dee.
Stalking Information: Mar Lodge Estate.
Tel: 03383-216/676.

Mountain: Carn na Drochaide, 2685ft/818m.
Map: OS Sheet 43: GR 127938.
Translation: hill of the bridge.
Pronunciation: kaarn na droch-itsh.
Access Point: Linn of Quoich, GR 117912.
Distance/ascent: 6mls/1650ft; 10km/503m.
Approx Time: 3-4 hours.
Route: Leave the wood and follow the track which leads in a NW direction above the Quoich Water. Follow the track after it narrows into a path and about the 550m contour leave it and take to the open slopes in a NE direction to the summit of Carn na Criche. From this summit follow the faint track ESE to the summit of Carn na Drochaide. Descend by the SW ridge to Allanquoich Farm.
Stalking Information: Mar Lodge Estate.
Tel: 03383-216/676.

Mountain: Creag an Dail Bheag (Carn Liath)
            2830ft/862m
            Culardoch, 2953ft/900m.
Map: OS Sheet 43: GR 158982, GR 194988.
Translation: small crag of the pasture, big back high place.
Pronunciation: krayk an daal bek, cul-aar-doch.
Access Point: Invercauld, GR 186916.
Distance/ascent: From Bealach Dearg, 5½mls/1900ft; 9km/579m.
Approx Time: 3-5 hours.
Route: From Invercauld either walk or use a bike to take the estate road which runs NW from the Keiloch sawmill. Take the first turning on the right before reach-

ing Invercauld House and follow this track uphill, initially through woods then open country for 3½mls/6km to the hut on the summit of the Bealach Dearg. From the hut, head ESE up the broad ridge to the summit of Carn Liath. Another summit, Creag an Dail Bheag about half a mile to the NE, is also given as 862m, but is one foot higher on the old one inch maps. Return to Carn Liath, then to the hut on the bealach. Follow the track up the SW ridge of Culardoch and where it turns to the left, leave it and head due E up steep slopes to the summit of Culardoch. Return the way you came.
Stalking Information: Invercauld Estate.
Tel: 03383-224/267.

20 Northern Cairngorms

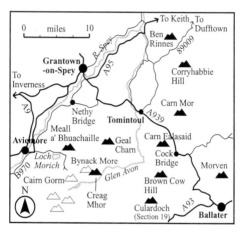

Suggested Base Accommodation	Grantown-on-Spey. Hotels, guest houses and b&b in Aviemore, Boat of Garten, Carrbridge, Nethybridge, Grantown-on-Spey and Tomintoul. Youth hostels in Aviemore, Loch Morlich and Tomintoul. Camp sites in Aviemore, Boat of Garten, and Grantown-on-Spey.
Public Transport	Rail: London, Glasgow and Edinburgh to Inverness. Stations at Aviemore and Carrbridge. Buses: London, Glasgow and Edinburgh via Perth to Inverness for Aviemore and Carrbridge.

The Cairngorms from the rocky summit of Creag Mhor

Mountain: Creag Mhor, 2936ft/895m.
Map: OS Sheet 36: GR 057048.
Translation: big crag.
Pronunciation: *krayk vor.*
Access Point: Glenmore Lodge, GR 986095.
Distance/ascent: 15mls/2500; 24km/762m.
Approx Time: 7-9hours.
Route: From the end of the road just past Glenmore Lodge follow the forestry track through the Pass of Ryvoan. Follow the sign post and track to Bynack Stable, cross the infant River Nethy and continue on the rough path which climbs onto the N ridge of Bynack More. Follow the path into Coire Odhar, past Bynack More and into the pass just N of Lochan a'Bhainne. From here leave the path and climb the slopes to the E, to the summit of Creag Mhor. Return the same way, or alternatively, descend the SW ridge to Fords of Avon bothy, follow the path W on the N bank of the River Avon before climbing to the Saddle at the head of Strath Nethy. Follow the Strath N to Bynack Stable.
Stalking Information: Abernethy Forest Lodge Estate.
Tel: 047982-619.

Mountain: Meall a'Bhuachaille, 2657ft/810m.
Map: OS Sheet 36: GR 991115.
Translation: hill of the shepherd.

Pronunciation: myowl a vooachil.
Access Point: Glenmore Lodge, GR 986095.
Distance/ascent: 5½mls/1600ft; 9km/488m.
Approx Time: 4-5 hours.
Route: Leave the public road just past Glenmore Lodge and follow the forestry track through the Pass of Ryvoan. Continue past the turn off to Bynack Stable and carry on until you reach Ryvoan Bothy. From here follow the path which runs W from behind the bothy up the E slopes of Meall a'Bhuachaille. Follow the path to the broad and stony summit. Descend W to the col between Meall a'Bhuachaille and Creagan Gorm and then S on the footpath which runs through the forest to Loch Morlich Youth Hostel.
Stalking Information: Abernethy Forest Lodge Estate.
Tel: 047982-619.

Mountain: Geal Charn, 2692ft/821m.
Map: OS Sheet 36: GR 090127.
Translation: white hill.
Pronunciation: gyal chaarn.
Access Point: Dorback Lodge, GR 080170.
Distance/ascent: 6mls/1650ft; 10km/503m.
Approx Time: 4-5 hours.
Route: From just W of Dorback Lodge a footpath runs S from the road to cross the Dorback Burn and continues to Upper Dell. From here take the bulldozed track S, past some small lochans, until it crosses the Allt nan Gamhuinn. From the junction of track and burn, ascend due S up the NE ridge of Geal Charn to the summit.
Stalking Information: Abernethy Forest Lodge.
Tel: 047982-619.

Mountain: Brown Cow Hill, 2721ft/829m.
Map: OS Sheet 36/37: GR 221044.
Pronunciation: as spelt.
Access Point: Corgarff Castle, Cock Bridge, GR 259087.
Distance/ascent: 12mls/1800ft; 20km/549m.
Approx Time: 5-7 hours.

Route: Leave the A939 road and follow the road which runs W alongside the infant River Don. Beyond Delnadamph Lodge at Inchmore, the track splits in two; take the left track and follow it through a plantation. As you leave the trees take to the open hill and climb the NE ridge of Cairn Culchavie to its summit. Continue SW past the Well of Don to Little Geal Charn, then SE to Meikle Geal Charn and Cairn Sawvie, and finally E over the broad plateau to Brown Cow Hill, the centre of three different tops. The OS name the E top as Brown Cow Hill, but it is 6m lower than the central top. Descend by the broad and peaty NE ridge to pick up the hill track to the SE of Carn Oighreag. Follow this track back to Cockbridge.

Stalking Information: Dalnadamph Estate (Balmoral Trustees).

Tel: 03384-334.

Mountain: Morven, 2877ft/877m.
Map: OS Sheet 37: GR 377040.
Translation: big hill.
Pronunciation: *more-ven.*
Access Point: Minor road between Bellabeg and Groddie, GR 410044.
Distance/ascent: 5mls/2200ft; 8km/670m.
Approx Time: 3-5 hours.
Route: Take the minor road which runs W from the A97 just S of Logie Coldstone. Follow this road for just over half a mile to where there is a parking place at a gate. Leaving your car, go through the gate and take the track which crosses some fields past the deserted farmhouse called Balhennie. Past the farmhouse take to the open hill beyond a wall, and climb to the E ridge of Morven. Follow the old fenceposts past a rocky outcrop and cairn to the summit. Return the same way.

Stalking Information: Balmoral Trustees.

Tel: 03384-334.

Mountain: Carn Ealasaid, 2600ft/792m
　　　　　　 Carn Mor, 2639ft/804m.
Map: OS Sheet 36/37: GR 2281188, GR 265183.

Heading towards Carn Mor on the Ladder Hills

Translation: Elizabeth's hill, big cairn.
Pronunciation: *kaarn yalasay, kaarn mor.*
Access Point: Car Park at Wells of Lecht, A939.
Distance/ascent: 14mls/2500ft; 23km/762m.
Approx Time: 5-7 hours.
Route: Leave the car park and follow the A939 W for
about a mile to Blairnamarrow. Just before you reach
the farm a gate gives access to a footpath which runs
SSE beside the Allt nan Cabar. Follow this path onto
the broad and very heathery N ridge which leads to a
col just W of Carn Ealasaid's summit. The path van-
ishes on this ridge, but follow the ridge to the col where
a SE direction will take you to the broad stony summit.
From the cairn, head N where you will pick up a bulldozed track which leads to a peaty col to the SW of
Beinn a'Chruinnich. From the col take a line which
skirts the S slopes of Beinn a'Chruinnich to the Lecht
ski slopes. Descend the slopes to the road just N of the
ski ground car park. From here, climb the steep slopes
on the E side of the road in a northerly diagonal line to
reach the N top of Meikle Corr Riabach (Pt 747m).
Follow the line of the fence N, NE, then N again to
Carn Liath, then NNE over Monadh an-Sluichd leith to
Carn Mor. Return to the long N ridge of Carn Liath,
and drop down deep heathery slopes into Coire Buidhe.
Follow the burn to the disused Ironstone Mine, then by
track to the car park at the Well of Lecht.
Stalking Information: Allargue Estate.
Tel: 09756-51448.

Mountain: Corryhabbie Hill, 2561ft/781m.

Map: OS Sheet 37: GR 281289.
Translation: unknown.
Pronunciation: *korrie-habbee.*
Access Point: Ellivreid Farm, GR 269325.
Distance/ascent: 7mls/1500ft; 11km/457m.
Approx Time: 3-5 hours.
Route: From the farm take the track on the opposite side of the road and follow it onto the NE ridge of Hill of Achmore. Follow this ridge on to Muckle Lapprach and then E to the summit of Corryhabbie Hill. Return by the NE ridge, dropping down the NW slopes to the ruins of the Falds of Cothabbie. From the ruins head NW to the track which runs to Ellivreid Farm.
Stalking Information: Glenlivet Estates.
Tel: 08073-201.

Mountain: Ben Rinnes, 2755ft/840m.
Map: OS Sheet 28: GR 255355.
Translation: headland hill.
Pronunciation: *byn reen-aysh.*
Access Point: Milltown of Edinvillie, B9009 Tomintoul to Dufftown road.
Distance/ascent: 4mls/2000ft; 6km/610m.
Approx Time: 3-5 hours.
Route: About a quarter of a mile beyond Milltown of Edinvillie take the track which climbs the slopes of Round Hill and beyond it, Roy's Hill. Continue due W on the well worn path to the summit of Ben Rinnes. Return the same way.
Stalking Information: Glenlivet Estates.
Tel: 08073-201.

21 Glen Roy, Laggan and Monadhliath

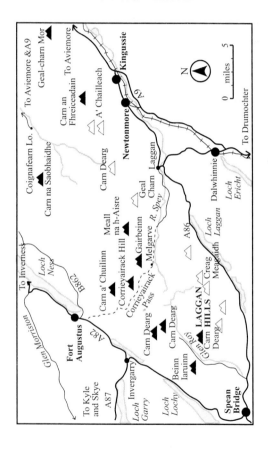

Suggested Base	Roybridge or Newtonmore.
Accommodation	Hotels, guest houses and b&b at Spean Bridge, Roybridge, Laggan and Newtonmore. Caravan sites at Roybridge and Newtonmore. Youth hostel at Kingussie. Private bunkhouses at Roybridge and Newtonmore. Camping/caravan site at Newtonmore.
Public Transport	Rail: London, Glasgow and Edinburgh to Inverness. Station at Newtonmore. Bus to Laggan, Roybridge and Fort William. Buses: London, Glasgow and Edinburgh to Inverness. Stops at Newtonmore.

Mountain: Geal-charn Mor, 2703ft/824m.
Map: OS Sheet 35: GR 837124.
Translation: big white hill.
Pronunciation: *gyal chaarn mor.*
Access Point: Lynwilg, GR 882107.
Distance/ascent: 7mls/2000ft; 12km/610m.
Approx Time: 4-6 hours.
Route: Follow the sign post to the Scripture Union Centre at Allt-na-Criche, and follow the track beside the burn. Bear right at the first junction and follow the estate road through the trees and onto the open hillside, continuing as far as a memorial on the high col. From there bear SW up the broad shoulder to the summit. Descend the same way, or alternatively, descend E to a footpath which runs S to Ballinluig Farm where tracks lead back to Lynwilg.
Stalking Information: Alvie Estate.
Tel: 05404-255.

Mountain: Carn an Fhreiceadain, 2879ft/878m.
Map: OS Sheet 35: GR 726071.
Translation: look-out cairn.
Pronunciation: *kaarn an raykat-yin.*
Access Point: Kingussie Golf Club car park.

Distance/ascent: 9mls/2000ft; 15km/610m.
Approx Time: 4-7 hours.
Route: Take the path behind the club house which leads to the tarmac road which runs N beside the river. Follow this road to Pitmain Lodge and turn right at the junction just before the footbridge. Follow this track through a gate, and up onto the hillside. The track stops just short of the summit of Beinn Bhreac. Pick up another track which runs W and follow it down to the col. Another bulldozed track now runs W to the summit of Carn an Fhreiceadain. Descend the hill by the same track, passing a large cairn, (the lookout cairn) on your right. Drop down to the path beside the Allt Mor and follow it back to Pitmain Lodge.
Stalking Information: Pitmain Estate.
Tel: 05402-661237.

Mountain: Carn a'Chuillin, 2677ft/816m.
Map: OS Sheet 34: GR 416034.
Translation: cairn of holly.
Pronunciation: *kaarn a hoolin.*
Access Point: A862, GR403090.
Distance/ascent: 7mls/2000ft; 12km/610m.
Approx Time: 4-6 hours.
Route: Follow the estate road S, past a lochan and up into Glen Doe. Around the 350m contour the track takes a tight twist – leave it at this point and follow the stalker's path onto the upper slopes. Continue S on the steeper slopes to the craggy summit. Return the same way.
Stalking Information: Glendoe Estate.
Tel: 0320-6203.

Mountain: Corrieyairack Hill, 2940ft/896m
                Gairbeinn, 2940ft/896m.
Map: OS Sheet 34: GR 429998, GR 460985.
Translation: hill of the rising glen, rough hill.
Pronunciation: *corrie-yare-ack, gaar-byn.*
Access Point: Melgarve, Corrieyairack Pass.
Distance/ascent: 9mls/2700ft; 15km/823m.
Approx Time: 4-7 hours.

Meall na h-Aisre from Garva Bridge

Route: Park at Melgarve and follow the route of the Corrieyairack Pass NW for 3mls/5km to just before the top of the pass. Leave the track and climb the slopes in a N direction to the summit of Corrieyairick Hill. Head E then SE to a narrow col above Loch Aonaich Odhair then up the slopes of Geal Charn. From the summit head due E, skirting the head of a corrie. Cross the peaty ground and climb on to the long ridge of Gairbeinn. Follow the rocky ridge in a SW direction to the summit cairn. Drop down steep slopes to the col to the NW of Meall a'Chuit and then down easy slopes back to Melgarve.

Stalking Information: British Alcan.

Tel: 0397-2433.

Mountain: Meall na h-Aisre, 2828ft/862m.

Map: OS Sheet 35: GR 515000.

Translation: hill of the defile.

Pronunciation: *myowl na hashra*.

Access Point: Garva Bridge.

Distance/ascent: 7mls/2100ft; 12km/640m.

Approx Time: 3-5 hours.

Route: Cross the bridge and take the path on the W bank of the Allt Coire Iain Oig. Follow this burn to its headwaters in Coire Iain Oig and climb the S slopes of

Carn Dearg of Glen Roy

the hill to its stony summit. Return by Leathad Gaothach to the Allt Coire Iain Oig and from there to Garva Bridge.
Stalking Information: British Alcan.
Tel: 0397-2433.

Mountain: Carn Dearg, 2675ft/815m
              Carn Dearg, 2520ft/768m.
Map: OS Sheet 34: GR 349967, GR 357948.
Translation: red cairn.
Pronunciation: kaarn jerrack.
Access Point: Near Brae Roy Lodge, Glen Roy.
Distance/ascent: 10mls/2700ft; 17km/823m.
*Approx Time:*5-7 hours.
Route: Follow the private road towards, then past Brae Roy Lodge and onto Turret Bridge. Immediately over the bridge take the track which forks off to the left and follow this to its end. Various tracks and paths now lead up Glen Turret and then into Gleann Eachach. At the mouth of this glen cross the Allt Eachach and take to the slopes of Teanga Mhor, the SW ridge of the most northerly of the two Carn Deargs. Climb the hill in a rising traverse in a NE direction to the summit. Descend in a SSE direction to the col between the two Carn Deargs and then climb, in much the same direction, to the summit of the second Carn Dearg. Descend back into Glen Turret by the SW ridge.

Stalking Information: Braeroy Estate c/o Finlayson Hughes, Inverness.
Tel: 0463-224343.

Mountain: Beinn Iaruinn, 2625ft/800m.
         Carn Dearg, 2763ft/842m.
Map: OS Sheet 34: GR 296900, GR 345887.
Translation: iron hill, red cairn.
Pronunciation: byn ee-ar-yin, kaarn jerrack.
Access Point: Glen Roy.
Distance/ascent: 10mls/4000ft; 16km/1219m.
Approx Time: 5-8 hours.
Route: These two hills can easily be climbed in one outing from Glen Roy. Start out for Carn Dearg from the bridge over the River Roy at GR 331909. Climb the slopes to the N of Coire na Reinich to the unamed summit and follow the broad ridge around the head of Coire na Reinich SSE to another top, then SSW to Carn Dearg. Descend in a NW direction to Carn Brunachan, then down that hill's N ridge back to Glen Roy. Head back down the road to a bridge over a stream at GR 308891 and climb Beinn Iaruinn by the ridge that bounds the S side of Coire nan Eun. From the top of the corrie cross a peaty plateau to reach the summit. Return the same way or continue around the top of Coire nan Eun, descending the very steep slopes on its N side.
Stalking Information: Braeroy Estate c/o Finlayson Hughes, Inverness.
Tel: 0463-224343.

Mountain: Carn na Saobhaidhe, 2660ft/811m.
Map: OS Sheet 35: GR 600145.
Translation: cairn of the fox's den.
Pronunciation: kaarn an sou-vey.
Access Point: Strath Nairn, B851 near the bridge over River Farigaig, GR 605246.
Distance/ascent: 15mls/2000ft; 26kms/610m.
Approx Time: 7-9 hours.
Route: Take the private road which leads to Dunmaglass Lodge. Just before the lodge a track forks to the left and leads to a footbridge over the River Farigaig. Fol-

low this track beside the Allt Uisg an t-Sidhein, taking the next track on the right below the slopes of Cairn beinn Mheadhoin. Higher up the glen another track leads off to the right so follow it to its termination high on the bare and bleak N slopes of Carn na Soabhaidhe. Continue in a S direction to the summit. Return the same way.

Stalking Information: Corriegarth Estate, c/o Savills,12 Clerk Street, Brechin, Angus, DD9 6AE. ***Tel:*** 0356-624184.

22 Loch Lochy, Loch Arkaig and Loch Eil

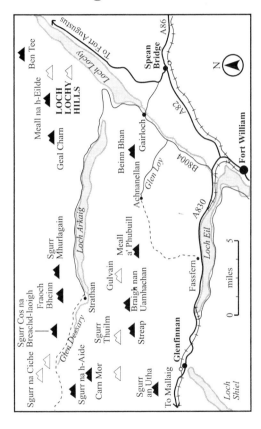

Suggested Base	Spean Bridge or Fort William.
Accommodation	Hotels, guest houses and b&b at Spean bridge, Fort William, Invergarry. Youth hostels at Fort William, (Glen Nevis) and Loch Lochy. Camping/caravan sites at Spean Bridge, Roybridge, Invergarry and Glen Nevis.
Public Transport	Rail: Glasgow to Mallaig. Stations at Spean bridge. Bus: Oban and Fort William to Inverness for Laggan Locks and Loch Lochy.

Mountain: Ben Tee, 2957ft/901m.
Map: OS Sheet 34: GR 241972.
Translation: faery hill.
Pronunciation: *byn tee.*
Access Point: Kilfinnan near Laggan Locks.
Distance/ascent: 5mls/2800ft; 8km/853m.
Approx Time: 4-6 hours.
Route: Follow the path which runs up the N side of the Kilfinnan Burn. Well before you reach the magnificent Kilfinnan Falls, take to the open hillside on the NE side of the stream and climb onto the wide open moorland above the glen. Take a WNW direction up the broad and featureless E ridge of Ben Tee and climb it to the narrowing, and increasingly rocky summit.
Stalking Information: Forestry Commission.
Tel: 0397-2184.

Mountain: Meall na h-Eilde, 2749ft/838m
                Geal Charn, 2638ft/804m.
Map: OS Sheet 34: GR 185946, GR 156943.
Translation: hill of the hinds, white cairn.
Pronunciation: *myowl na hale-dya, gyal chaarn.*
Access Point: Eas-Chia-aig, near Achnacarry.
Distance/ascent: 11mls/3400ft; 18km/1036m.
Approx Time: 6-8 hours.
Route: The Eas-Chia-aig is a fine waterfall at the west end of the Mile Dorcha on the B8005. From the parking place, follow the footpath which climbs steeply up

---

through the forest. This path soon joins up with a forestry track which runs N up Gleann Cia-aig. Follow the track through the forest and a short distance after leaving the trees you'll find a footbridge over the river. Ignore this one and continue N to the next footbridge at the junction of two streams. Cross the bridge and climb the slopes to the W of the Bealach an Easain to the summit of Meall na h-Eilde. Descend NW to the Bealach Choire a'Ghuirein and climb the obvious ridge W to the summit of Meall Coire nan Saobhaidh. Descend easy slopes in a SW direction to the Bealach Carn na h-Urchaire and its small lochan, and then climb the steepening slopes SW to Geal Charn. Descend the SE ridge to the stalker's path which follows the Allt Dubh S to Achnasaul. Follow the road 1½ mls/2.4km back to Eas-Chia-aig.

Stalking Information: Locheil Estates.
Tel: 0397-2433.

Mountain: Sgurr Mhurlagain, 2886ft/880m
　　　　　　Fraoch Bheinn, 2815ft/858m
　　　　　　Sgurr Cos na Breachd-laoigh,
　　　　　　2739ft/835m.
Map: OS Sheet 33/40: GR 012944, GR 986940, GR 948947.
Translation: peak of the bay-shaped inlet, heathery hill, peak of the cave of the bonny calf.
Pronunciation: *skoor voor-lagin, froe-ch vyn, skoor cos na brecht loo-ee.*
Access Point: Strathan, GR 980915.
Distance/ascent: 12mls/6000ft; 20km/1829m.
Approx Time: 7-10 hours.
Route: From Strathan follow the landrover track towards Glen Dessarry for a short distance then head NE up the stalker's path beside the Dearg Allt to the 500m contour. From here strike E up slopes which lead to the SW ridge of Sgurr Mhurlagain and follow it to the steepening slopes which lead to the summit. Descend to the bealach between Sgurr Mhurlagain and Fraoch Bheinn abd climb steepening slopes to the W, avoiding the rocky outcrops, to reach the SW ridge. Follow this ridge to the summit. From the top, descend the SW ridge for 3-400m until you can descend W, avoiding the rocky out-

crops, into the glen above Glendessary Lodge. Cross the glen and gain the SE ridge of Druim a'Chuirn. Follow the ridge to the top and follow the fine horseshoe ridge SW to Sgurr Cos na Breachd-laoigh. Descend to Glendessary Lodge by the SE ridge, then by track to Strathan.

Stalking Information: Locheil Estates for Sgurr Mhurlagain, tel: 0397-2433. Forestry Commission, tel: 0397-2184.

Mountain: Sgurr na h-Aide, 2844ft/867m.
Map: OS Sheet 33: GR 8889931.
Translation: peak of the hawk (peak of the hat).
Pronunciation: *skoor na haatch.*
Access Point: Strathan, GR 980915.
Distance/ascent: 13mls/3000ft; 21km/914m.
Approx Time: 7-9 hours.
Route: Either walk, or preferably cycle along the track to Glen Dessary and take the forestry track on the south side of the glen. At the junction of the River Dessary and the Allt Coire nan Uth, cross the Dessary by the rather primitive bridge and gain the right of way which leads to Loch Nevis over the mam na Cloich Airde. Continue along the right of way for about half a mile, cross the headwaters of the River Dessary and climb the slopes W to Meall na Sroine. Continue W along the knobbly ridge which leads to Druim Coire nan Laogh and along that ridge to the steepening slopes which lead to the summit. The slopes to the N and the S are very tricky, with rocky crags and slabs, so descend the route of ascent to Glen Dessary.
Stalking Information: Glendessary Estate.
Tel: 039785-251.

Mountain: Carn Mor, 2719ft/829m.
Map: OS Sheet 33: GR 903910.
Translation: big cairn.
Pronunciation: *kaarn mor.*
Access Point: Strathan, GR 980915.
Distance/ascent: 10mls/2600ft; 17km/792m.
Approx Time: 6-8 hours.

Route: Take the forestry track on the S side of Glen Dessarry as far as A'Chuil Bothy. Beyond the bothy a gap in the forestry gives access to the long E ridge of Carn Mor. Follow the long and undulating ridge to the summit. Return the same way.
Stalking Information: Glendessary Estate.
Tel: 039785-251.

Mountain: Meall a'Phubuill, 2539ft/774m.
Map: OS Sheet 41: GR 029854.
Translation: hill of the tent.
Pronunciation: *myowl a foo-beel.*
Access Point: Fassfern, A830, GR 022789.
Distance/ascent: 9mls/2500ft; 15km/762m.
Approx Time: 6-8 hours.
Route: From the minor road at Fassfern walk or preferably cycle up the track on the E bank of the Ant t-Suileag. Follow this track N through the forest and beyond it to Glensulaig on the N bank of the river. Climb Meall a'Phubuill by its S slopes. Return the same way.
Stalking Information: Locheil Estates.
Tel: 0397-2433.

Mountain: Beinn Bhan, 2612ft/796m.
Map: OS Sheet 41: GR 141857.
Translation: white hill.
Pronunciation: *byn vaan.*
Access Point: Inverskilavulin, GR 126835.
Distance/ascent: 5mls/2500ft; 8km/762m.
Approx Time: 4-6 hours.
Route: From Inverskilavulin climb the slopes between the fence and the burn N to the edge of Coire Mhuilinn. Follow the corrie rim over the two 771m tops and then SE to the summit trig point. Descend WSW then S, gradually heading SW to the corrie edge and back down beside the burn.
Stalking Information: Locheil Estates.
Tel: 0397-2433.

Streap from Sgurr Thuilm

Mountain: Braigh nan Uamhachan, 2510ft/765m.
Map: OS Sheet 40: GR 975867.
Translation: slope of the caves.
Pronunciation: brae nan oo-avochan.
Access Point: A830, GR 799931.
Distance/ascent: 9mls/2800ft; 14km/853m.
Approx Time: 6-8 hours.
Route: Follow the forest road up Gleann Dubh Lighe
to half a mile or so beyond the Dubh Lighe Bothy. Here,
on the edge of the forestry plantation head NE up the
SW slopes of Na h-Uamhachan to its top. From this top
follow the ridge over Sron Liath alongside a substan-
tial wall to the summit of Braigh nan Uamhachan. Re-
turn the same way or drop down the E slopes into Gleann
Fionnlighe and S to the A830.
Stalking Information: Locheil Estates.
Tel: 0397-2433.

Mountain: Streap, 2982ft/909m.
Map: OS Sheet 40: GR 946863.
Translation: climbing hill.
Pronunciation: strehp.
Access Point: A830, GR 975867.
Distance/ascent: 9mls/3800ft; 14km/1158m.
Approx Time: 6-8 hours.
Route: As in the route above, follow the forestry track
to a point opposite the Dubh Lighe Bothy. Continue on
the track to the open hillside above the forestry. Con-

tinue on the open slopes in a NW direction to reach the col between Beinn an Tuim and Stob Coire nan Cearc. Head NE over the rocky undulating ridge over the 844m point, down to the col below Streap then over the knife edge ridge which leads to the summit of Streap. Descend in a SE direction and climb a short distance to Streap Comhlaidh. From here descend the S ridge to the forest track which runs S past the bothy to the A830.
Stalking Information: Locheil Estates.
Tel: 0397-2433.

Mountain: Sgurr an Utha, 2610ft/796m.
Map: OS Sheet 40: GR 885839.
Translation: peak of the udder.
Pronunciation: skoor an oo-a.
Access Point: A830, GR 875817.
Distance/ascent: 4mls/2500ft; 6km/762m.
Approx Time: 3-5 hours.
Route: About a mile W of Glenfinnan, the A830 Fort William to Mallaig road crosses over the Allt Feith a'Chata. Just E of the bridge a forestry track runs N beside the stream and carries you through the forestry plantation and onto the open hill beyond. After about half a mile the track veers to the NE, following the course of the Allt an Utha. Leave the track at about the 300m contour, cross the stream and climb the SW ridge of Sgurr an Utha. (There is a footbridge at the confluence of the Allt an Utha and the Allt feith a'Chata - useful in spate conditions.) Climb the rocky ridge over a number of bumps and knolls to the summit. As an alternative descent, drop down in a WSW direction to the col and climb Fraoch-bheinn, then descend its SW ridge to Druim na Brein-choille to pick up the forest track you left earlier.
Stalking Information: Glenfinnan Estate.
Tel: 039783-270.

22(a) Ardgour, Moidart and Loch Shiel

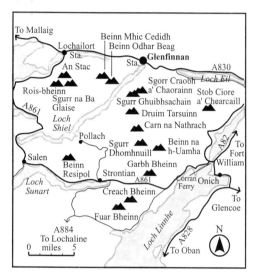

Suggested Base	Glenfinnan or Strontian.
Accommodation	Hotels and b&b at Glenfinnan, Strontian, Acharacle, Lochailort, and Glenuig. Camping/caravan sites at Srontian, and at Back of Keppoch.(Arisaig).
Public Transport	Rail: Glasgow to Mallaig (West Highland Line) Buses: Glasgow and Edinburgh to Skye for Corran. Ferry to Ardgour for once-a-day bus service to Kilchoan in Ardnamurchan. Ferry from Fort William to Camusnagaul.

Mountain: Fuar Bheinn, 2510ft/765m
Creach Bheinn,2798ft/853m.
Map: OS Sheet 49: GR 853564, GR 871577.
Translation: cold hill, hill of spoil.
Pronunciation: foo-ur vyn, krech vyn.
Access Point: Bridge over Galmadale River, B8043.
Distance/ascent: 10mls/4950ft; 17km/1508m.
Approx Time: 6-9 hours.
Route: Leave the road just after it turns SW and climb
the steep hill beside a forestry plantation to reach the
grassy SE ridge of Beinn na Cille. From the top de-
scend in a NNW direction to a col and then climb the
long and broad S ridge of Fuar Bheinn. Descend NW
then N to the Cul Mham, and then continue up the stony
W ridge of Creach Bheinn. Descend a rocky and nar-
row ridge in a NE direction, then bear E and eventually
SE across the bealach at the head of Coire Dhuibh to
the summit of Maol Odhar. Continue from the top in a
SE direction and either drop down into Glengalmadale
or continue around the horseshoe, climbing Meall nan
Each before descending down the long bumpy ridge of
Druim na Maodalaich to the B8043.
Stalking Information: Forestry Commission.
Tel: 0397-2184.

Mountain: Garbh Bheinn, 2903ft/885m.
Map: OS Sheet 40: GR 904622.
Translation: rough mountain.
Pronunciation: gara-vyn.
Access Point: Bridge over the Abhainn Coire an Iubhair,
A861.
Distance/ascent: 6mls/2900ft; 10km/884m.
Approx Time: 5-7 hours.
Route: From the bridge climb the open slopes on the
W side of the Abhainn Coire an Iubhair which lead to
the long Sron a'Garbh Choire Bhig. Ascend this ridge
to its summit, descend the rocky NW ridge to the col
and continue N up steep and rocky slopes to gain the
summit ridge just W of the summit. Return by descend-
ing to the col below Sron a'Garbh Choire Bhig, then
contiinue the descent, this time in a NE direction down

steep and rocky slopes to the head of Coire an Iubhair. A path on the E bank of the burn leads back to the starting point.

Stalking Information: Ardgour Estate.
Tel: 08555-247.

Mountain: Beinn Resipol, 2772ft/845m.
Map: OS Sheet 40: GR 766655.
Translation: from the Norse – homestead mountain.
Pronunciation: *byn ray-sha-pol.*
Access Point: Resipole, A 861, GR 722643.
Distance/ascent: 6mls/2800ft; 10km/853m.
Approx Time: 4-6 hours.
Route: From the farm at Resipole follow the track N. After a short distance the track degenerates into a footpath and this can be followed up the SE bank of the Allt Mhic Chiarain. Continue through woodland and onto the open hill beyond where the path eventually disappears but keep following the burn in an E direction and just before it meets with Lochan Bac an Lochain cross to its N bank and climb the W ridge of Beinn Resipol to it's summit. Return the same way or, if transport can be arranged, traverse the mountain, descending by its SE slopes over Meall an t-Slugain to pick up the old miner's path which leads down to Ariundle, N of Strontian.

Stalking Information: Sunart Estate, DAFS, Estates Management, Chesser House, Gorgie Road, Edinburgh, EH11 3AW.
Tel: 031-339-8319.

Mountain: Sgurr Dhomhnuill, 2914ft/888m.
Map: OS Sheet 40: GR 889679.
Translation: Donald's peak.
Pronunciation: *skoor ghaw-il.*
Access Point: Ariundle Nature Reserve car park.
Distance/ascent: 8mls/3600ft; 13km/1097m.
Approx Time: 6-8 hours.
Route: From the car park walk up the glen taking the upper path which eventually leads to the old Feith Dhomhnuill lead mines. From the end of the path cross

the stream to its E bank and climb the slopes to the NE to gain the Druim Leac a'Sgiathain. Follow this E onto the ridge leading to Sgurr na h-Ighinn then NE to a col, before ascending the final slopes N to the trig point on Sgurr Dhomhnuill. Descend in a NW direction to a col, then climb to the 803m point, the end of the Druim Garbh. Descend this ridge, eventually dropping off SW to reach the lead mines and the Nature Trail path.

Stalking Information: Sunart Estate, DAFS Estates Management, Chesser House, Gorgie Road, Edinburgh EH11 3AW.
Tel: 031-339-8319.

Mountain: Carn na Nathrach, 2579ft/786m.
Map: OS Sheet 40: GR 887699.
Translation: cairn of the snakes.
Pronunciation: *kaarn na-trach*.
Access Point: Kinlochan, GR 819674.
Distance/ascent: 10mls/2600ft; 16km/792m.
Approx Time: 5-7 hours.
Route: Walk along the forestry road in Glen Hurich to the footbridge over the River Hurich. Continue E once over the bridge and cross the Alltan Dubh Chorein. Continue on this track as it bends NE then S and as it crosses the bottom of the Beinn Mheadhoin ridge, strike NE through the trees to the open hillside. Follow the bumpy ridge for about 2½mls/4km to the narrower section which leads to the summit of Carn na Nathrach. Return the same way as forestry severely limits the other options.
Stalking Information: Forestry Commission.
Tel: 0397-2184.

Mountain: Beinn na h-Uamha, 2500ft/762m.
Map: OS Sheet 40: GR 917664.
Translation: hill of the caves.
Pronunciation: *byn na oo-ava*.
Access Point: Sallachan, A861.
Distance/ascent: 9mls/2600ft; 14km/792m.
Approx Time: 5-7 hours.

Route: Follow the track on the S side of Glen Gour, passing the S shore of Loch nan Gabhar and the ruins at Tigh Ghlinnegabhar. About a mile beyond the ruins cross the river to its N bank (could be difficult under spate conditions) and climb the SE ridge of Beinn na h-Uamha. This is a rocky ridge, with many false tops and bumps. Follow the ridge to the summit. Return by the same route, although a fine traverse can be made of the mountain by continuing to Sgurr a'Chaorainn and then descending to the Ariundle Nature Trail at Strontian.
Stalking Information: Ardgour Estate.
Tel: 08555-247.

Mountain: Druim Tarsuinn, 2525ft/770m.
Map: OS Sheet 40: GR 854727.
Translation: transverse ridge.
Pronunciation: drim tars-in.
Access Point: Callop cottage, 1 mile E of Glenfinnan.
Distance/ascent: 12mls/2900ft; 20km/883m.
Approx Time: 6-8 hours.
Route: Cross the bridge over the Callop River and follow the path S past Callop cottage and up the W bank of the Allt na-Cruaiche. Continue on the footpath in a SW direction for about 2½mls/4km until the path splits in two where it overlooks the Cona Glen. Take the right branch of the path in a WSW direction and follow it into the head of the Cona Glen, where easy slopes lead W to the start of the Druim Tarsuinn ridge. Follow the ridge over the Bealach an Sgriodain to the summit of the Corbett. (The SMC have suggested that this top be named Stob a'Bhealach an Sgriodain, rather than Druim Tarsuinn which they point out is only the name of the ridge leading to the bealach). Descend E down a rocky ridge to the col between the summit and Meall Mor, and from there NE then N to the River Cona. In times of spate it's best to descend by the way you came, ie, by the head of the Cona Glen. From the river climb the slopes to the N, pick up the footpath, and follow it back to Callop.
Stalking Information: Cona Glen Estate.
Tel: 0397-2433.

Mountain: Sgurr Ghiubhsachain, 2784ft/849m
Sgorr Craobh a'Chaorainn, 2543ft/775m.
Map: OS Sheet 40: GR 875752, GR 896757.
Translation: peak of the fir wood, peak of the rowan tree.
Pronunciation: *skoor choov-shachan, skoor kroove-a chou-ran.*
Access Point: Bridge over the Callop River, E of Glenfinnan.
Distance/ascent: 10mls/3500ft; 16km/1067m.
Approx Time: 6-8 hours.
Route: Take the forestry road which runs from the bridge in a NW direction and follow it for 3mls/5km to the cottage of Guesachan on the shore of Loch Shiel. Follow the Allt Coire Ghiubhsachain into its corrie for some distance to avoid the lower rocky slopes of Sgurr Ghiubhsachain, then climb onto the ridge, which is steep and rocky. Continue over Meall a'Choire Chruinn and climb the final ridge to the first of two summits. A level ridge leads to the highest one. Descend the E ridge, a mixture of rocky slabs and grass to a small lochan on the col. From there follow the ridge in a NE direction, bypassing any rocky difficulties on the right, to the summit of Sgorr Craobh a'Chaorainn. Descend in a NE direction over Meall na Cuartaige to join the footpath which leads back to Callop.
Stalking Information: Cona Glen Estate.
Tel: 0397-2433.

Mountain: Stob Coire a'Chearcaill, 2528ft/771m.
Map: OS Sheet 41: GR 107727.
Translation: peak of the circular corrie.
Pronunciation: *stop cora a chyar-kal.*
Access Point: Stroncheggan, A861.
Distance/ascent: 7mls/2600ft; 11km/792m.
Approx Time: 4-6 hours.
Route: Follow the track which leads W through grazing fields for just over a mile to a gate which leads onto open country. Pass through the gate and climb the slopes onto the Braigh Bhlaich ridge. Follow the crest of the

ridge, round the N facing corrie, to the large cairn which is slightly higher than the trig point. Return the same way.
Stalking Information: Cona Glen Estate.
Tel: 0397-2433.

Mountain: Beinn Odhar Beag, 2895ft/882m
Beinn Mhic Cedidh, 2569ft/783m.
Map: OS Sheet 40: GR 846778, GR 828787.
Translation: small dun-coloured hill, MacCedidh's hill.
Pronunciation: *byn oo-er bayk, byn vik kee-ya*.
Access Point: Car park at E end of Loch Eilt.
Distance/ascent: 7mls/4100ft; 12km/1250m.
Approx Time: 5-7 hours.
Route: Cross the Allt Lon a'Mhuidhe by the stepping stones a couple of hundred yards E of Loch Eilt. Once across the river follow the railway line W to the bridge over the Allt a'Choin Bhuidhe. Cross the river by the railway bridge to its W bank and ascend the slopes which lead to a col at the foot of the N ridge of Beinn Mhic Cedidh. Follow this ridge, which becomes narrower and rockier the higher you climb, to the summit. Drop down the slopes to the E to the Bealach a'Choire Bhuidhe and climb the NW ridge of Beinn Odhar Bheag to its summit. Follow the N ridge to reach Beinn Odhar Mhor, then descend its NW ridge to the lower reaches of the Allt a'Choin Bhuidhe. Cross the railway and return to your starting point.
Stalking Information: Inverailort Estate, Inverailort Castle, Inverailort.
Tel: 06877-247.

Mountain: Rois-Bheinn, 2895ft/882m
Sgurr na Ba Glaise, 2867ft/874m
An Stac, 2671ft/814m.
Map: OS Sheet 40: GR 756778, GR 771777, GR 763794.
Translation: showery hill, peak of the grey cow, the stack.
Pronunciation: *rosh-vyn, skoor na ba glasha, an stak*.
Access Point: Inverailort.

Rois-Bheinn from Sgurr na Ba Glaise

Distance/ascent: 10mls/4800ft; 16km/1463m.
Approx Time: 6-8 hours.
Route: Take the farm track which runs ENE from
Inverailort and cross the burn which issues from the
low col between the hillock of Tom Odhar and the NE
ridge of Seann Chruach. Follow the footpath through
the col and onto open moorland. Continue S up Coire
a'Bhuiridh, before crossing to the E bank of the Allt
a'Bhuiridh. Climb the W slopes of Beinn Coire nan
Gall, making for the col between it and Druim Fiaclach.
Climb to the summit of Druim Fiaclach by its steep N
ridge. Follow the SW ridge of this hill to a small col,
and then continue S over another bump to a fine high
level lochan. Continue WSW on this fine ridge, over a
subsidiary top, then onto the summit of Sgurr na Ba
Glaise. Descend steep slopes to the Bealach an Fhiona
before following an old wall up steep and rocky slopes
to the E top and trig point of Rois-Bheinn. Return to
the Bealach an Fhiona, descend more steep and rocky
slopes to the N and climb more steep slopes to the summit of An Stac. Descend N, then NNE down rocky
slopes to Seann Cruach, then down its NE ridge to the
woods above the Tom Odhar col. Go through the woods
to the col, and make your way back to Inverailort.
Stalking Information: Inverailort Estate, Inverailort
Castle, Inverailort.
Tel: 06877-247.

23 Knoydart and Loch Quoich

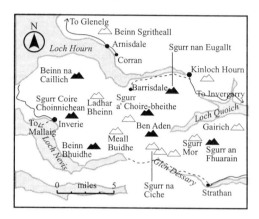

Suggested Base Accommodation	Kinloch Hourn or Inverie. B&B at Kinloch Hourn and Inverie. Hotels, guest houses and b&b at Invergarry, Spean Bridge, Sheil Bridge and Tomdoun. Private hostel at Inverie.
Public Transport	Rail: Glasgow to Mallaig. Stations at Spean Bridge and Fort William for onward bus services. Mallaig for ferry to Inverie. Buses: Glasgow to Skye. Edinburgh and Perth to Skye for Invergarry. Fort William to Inverness for Invergarry. Post Buses: Invergarry to Kinloch Hourn for Loch Quoich-side. Kyle of Lochalsh to Arnisdale for ferry to Barrisdale on Knoydart. Ferries: Arnisdale to Kinloch Hourn for Barrisdale, Mallaig to Inverie on Loch Nevis.

Mountain: Sgurr an Fhuarain, 2956ft/901m.
Map: OS Sheet 33: GR 987980.
Translation: possibly Oran's peak.
Pronunciation: *skoor an oo-a-ran.*
Access Point: Strathan.
Distance/ascent: 10mls/3300ft; 16km/1006m.
Approx Time: 6-8 hours.
Route: From Strathan follow the track into Glen Dessary as far as Glendessary Lodge. From there, follow the footpath N into and over the pass of the Feith a'Chicheanais. Once over the pass leave the footpath, continue down hill and cross the River Kingie. In high river conditions cross as far W as possible. Once you are N of the Kingie, climb the steep slopes to the col between Sgurr Mor and Sgurr an Fhuaran, then E along the ridge to the summit. A good alternative which takes in the Munro of Sgurr Mor is to cross the Kingie, and follow the good stalker's path which runs W. This soon cuts back on itself and climbs Sgurr Beag then Sgurr Mor. Follow the path over the summits, down to the col E of Sgurr Mor and then along the ridge to the Corbett.
Stalking Information: Forestry Commission.
Tel: 0397-2184.

Mountain: Ben Aden, 2910ft/887m.
Map: OS Sheet 33: GR 899986.
Translation: hill of the face.
Pronunciation: *byn aa-din.*
Access Point: Sourlies bothy, GR 869951.
Distance/ascent: 10mls/3000ft; 16km/910m.
Approx Time: 6-8 hours.
Route: This is an extremely remote hill and there is no quick and easy approach to it. Possibly the simplest route is from Sourlies bothy at the E end of Loch Nevis. Follow the River Carnoch to its confluence with the Allt Achadh a'Ghlinne. From there thread your way up the SW face of the hill avoiding the steep crags and outcrops. As you climb higher pull more to the N to avoid the very steep ground below the summit. Once you reach the NW ridge, follow it to the summit. An alternative, but longer route from Barrisdale in the N,

follows the path through Gleann Unndalain to the E
end of Lochan nam Breac. Continue E on the footpath
for a short distance then follow the Allt Coire Cruaiche
S and SW to reach Ben Aden's E ridge. Follow this
steeply to the summit. You can also reach Lochan nam
Breac from the W end of Loch Quoich.
Stalking Information: Camusrory Estate.
Tel: 0687-2342.

Mountain: Sgurr a'Choire-beithe, 2994ft/913m.
Map: OS Sheet 33: GR 895015.
Translation: peak of the corrie of birch trees.
Pronunciation: *skoor a cora bay.*
Access Point: Barrisdale.
Distance/ascent: 6mls/3100ft; 9km/945m.
Approx Time: 4-6 hours.
Route: Follow the path which runs S into Gleann
Unndalain, past some ruins and up the initial slopes of
Doire Asamaidh. As the path turns SE into the steeply
enclosed pass take to the open hill and follow the WNW
ridge of Sgurr a'Choire-beithe which rises steadily to a
prominent, but false, summit. The true summit is a short
distance beyond.
Stalking Information: Barrisdale Estate.
Tel: 079681-240.

Mountain: Sgurr nan Eugallt, 2933ft/912m.
Map: OS Sheet 33: GR 931045.
Translation: peak of death streams.
Pronunciation: *skoor nan egg-ault.*
Access Point: Coireshubh, GR 958054.
Distance/ascent: 6mls/2900ft; 9km/884m.
Approx Time: 4-6 hours.
Route: Start from the ruined cottage at Coireshubh,
(corrie of the raspberries) and follow the excellent stalk-
er's path due W then SW onto the NW ridge at the col
between the summit and Sgurr Dubh. From the col fol-
low the ridge SW to the summit. A good alternative
descent is to traverse the main ridge to Sgurr

a'Chlaidheimh, then descend to the NE down steep and slabby slopes which shouldn't provide any great difficulty if the weather is clear.
Stalking Information: Wester Glen Quoich Estate.
Tel: 079681-240.

Mountain: Beinn Bhuidhe, 2805ft/855m.
Map: OS Sheet 33; GR 822967.
Translation: yellow hill.
Pronunciation: *byn voo-ee.*
Access Point: Inverie.
Distance/ascent: 12mls/3400ft; 20km/1036m.
Approx Time: 7-10 hours.
Route: From Inverie, take the Mam Barrisdale road from the village, but beyond the monument at GR 793990 cross the Inverie River and follow the footpath which leads to the Mam Meadail. From the high point of the pass leave the footpath and climb the slopes to the SW to Meall Bhasiter. Descend W to the Mam Uchd, and from there follow the ridge W to the summit of Beinn Bhuidhe. Continue W to Sgurr Coire nan Gobhar, descend to Loch Bhraomisaig, then NE to the bridge over the Inverie River.
Stalking Information: Knoydart Estate.
Tel: 0687-2000.

Mountain: Sgurr Coire Choinnichean, 2612ft/796m.
Map: OS Sheet 33; GR 791011.
Translation: peak of the mossy corrie.
Pronunciation: *skoor cora chon-yeech-an.*
Access Point: Inverie.
Distance/ascent: 5mls/2600ft; 8km/792m.
Approx Time: 4-6 hours.
Route: Take the road N from the village school which leads eventually to the Mam Uidhe. Once you are clear of the forest, head E up open slopes to the open, level Coire Choinnichean. At the S end of this flat area there is a prominent gorge which contains the Alltt Slocha a' Mhogha. Pass this in a SE direction to gain the lower part of the SW ridge. Follow this ridge NE to the sum-

mit. An alternative descent follows the ridge NE to the col, then drops down E to the Gleann an Dubh-Lochain track. This is then followed back to Inverie.
Stalking Information: Knoydart Estate.
Tel: 0687-2000.

Mountain: Beinn na Caillich, 2575ft/785m.
Map: OS Sheet 33: GR 796067.
Translation: hill of the old woman.
Pronunciation: *byn na kalyeech.*
Access Point: Inverie.
Distance/ascent: 12mls/2900ft; 20km/884m.
Approx Time: 6-9 hours.
Route: Take the Mam Uidhe track from Inverie for about 1½mls/2.4km then head NE on another track which runs into Gleann na Guiserein. Continue E to the footbridge at Folach, cross the river, and follow the stalker's path NNE to the summit of the Mam Li. Follow the E ridge of Beinn na Caillich to the summit. From the cairn, descend SW along the ridge to Meall Coire an t-Searraich, then down the SE slopes back to Gleann na Guiserein.
Stalking Information: Knoydart Estate.
Tel: 0687-2000.

24 The Glen Shiel Hills

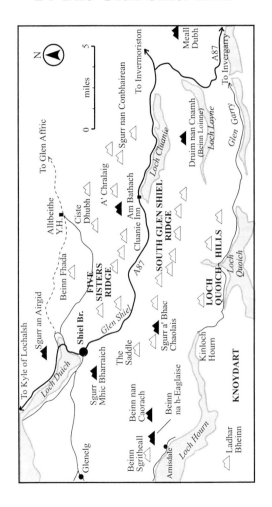

Suggested Base	Shiel Bridge.
Accommodation	Hotels, guest houses, b&b at Shiel Bridge, Dornie, Cluanie and Glenelg. Youth hostel at Ratagan.
Public Transport	Rail: Inverness to Kyle of Lochalsh for onward bus services. Buses: Kyle of Lochalsh and Plockton to Shiel Bridge and Letterfearn. Glasgow and Fort William to Skye, all stopping at Shiel Bridge. Post Buses: Kyle of Lochalsh to Arnisdale for Shiel Bridge.

Mountain: Meall Dubh, 2585ft/788m.
Map: OS Sheet 34: GR 245078.
Translation: black hill.
Pronunciation: *myowl doo*.
Access Point: A87, Loch Loyne dam.
Distance/ascent: 5mls/1700ft; 8km/518m.
Approx Time: 3-5 hours.
Route: Leave the car park which is situated close to the Loch Loyne dam. Cross the road and follow the slopes E, just S of the Garbh Dhoire forest. Follow the course of the Allt Bealach Odhair as far as possible then continue E to the summit. Two cairns grace the top; the smaller one is the true summit.
Stalking Information: Forestry Commission.
Tel: 0397-2184.

Mountain: Druim nan Cnamh, 2592ft/790m.
Map: OS Sheet 34: GR 131077.
Translation: bony ridge.
Pronunciation: *drim nan kraav*.
Access Point: A87, Loch Loyne dam.
Distance/ascent: 10mls/2600ft; 16km/792m.
Approx Time: 5-7 hours.
Route: Druim nan Cnamh is, strictly speaking, the name of the ridge to the S of the E end of Loch Cluanie, the highest point which is unnamed on the OS map. Beinn Loinne is the middle summit of this ridge and the west-

ern summit, the highest, has been christened Beinn
Loinne (west peak) by the SMC. Most walkers still re-
fer to it as Druim nan Cnamh.

From the dam at the NE end of Loch Loyne head W
across wet and boggy rising moorland to reach the SE
slopes of the Druim nan Cnamh. Climb the steepening
slopes to the ridge E of Beinn Loinne. Cross this top
and continue W to the trig point. Return the same way.
An alternative route, which avoids the boggy moorland
W of Loch Loyne but gives a lot of road walking is to
take the old road from Cluanie Inn which runs to
Tomdoun. From the highest point on the road go E across
more boggy ground. The going improves as you come
closer to the summit.

Stalking Information: Forestry Commission.
Tel: 0397-2184.

Mountain: Sgurr a'Bhac Chaolais, 2904ft/885m.
Map: OS Sheet 33: GR 958110.
Translation: peak of the hollow of the narrows.
Pronunciation: skoor a vach choul-ash.
Access Point: Bridge over the Allt Mhalagain, Glen
Shiel.
Distance/ascent: 7mls/3300ft; 11kms/1006m.
Approx Time: 5-8 hours.
Route: Follow the track S beside the Allt Mhalagain
into Glen Toteil. Keep to the path which climbs quite
steeply and follow the zigzags, indistinct in places,
which lead to the Bealach Duibh Leac. From the pass,
bear WSW following the direction of an old wall and
fenceposts over an undulating ridge to the summit of
Sgurr a'Bhac Chaolais. To complete a fine round of
Coire Toteil, continue W from the summit down to the
bealach SE of Sgurr na Sgine. Take care here for the S
facing slopes of Sgurr na Sgine are very steep and loose.
Best to traverse rightwards to gain the foot of the E
ridge and ascend that to the summit. From the summit
of the Munro follow the long ridge round the head of
Coire Toteil, over Faochag and then down to Glen Shiel.
Stalking Information: Cluanie Estate.
Tel: 059981-282.

Mountain: Beinn na h-Eaglaise, 2641ft/805m
             Beinn nan Caorach, 2904ft/885m.
Map: OS Sheet 33: GR 854120, GR 871122.
Translation: hill of the church, hill of the rowan berries.
Pronunciation: byn na hyuk-leesha, byn nan koe-roch.
Access Point: Arnisdale.
Distance/ascent: 10mls/3500ft; 17km/1067m.
Approx Time: 5-7 hours.
Route: Take the track W from Arnisdale up Glen
Arnisdale to a bridge over the river. Go N, past the cottage at Achad a'Ghlinne and follow the stalker's path
which follows the E bank of the Allt Utha. Just beyond
the falls of Eas na Cuingid leave the path and follow
the SSW ridge of Beinn nan Caorach all the way to the
summit. Head N, the NW along a line of old fence posts
to the head of Coire Dhruim nan Bo. Continue W onto
the ridge itself, descend SW to another bealach then
climb the impressive NE shoulder of Beinn na h-
Eaglaise, following the narrowing ridge all the way to
the summit. Descend to Arnisdale by way of Beinn
Bhuidhe, the SSW to the track in Glen Arnisdale.
Stalking Information: Arnisdale Estate.
Tel: 059982-216.

Mountain: Sgurr Mhic Bharraich, 2561ft/781m.
Map: OS Sheet 33: GR 917174.
Translation: peak of the son of Maurice.
Pronunciation: skoor vic var-rach.
Access Point: Campsite at Shiel Bridge.
Distance/ascent: 5mls/2500ft; 8km/762m.
Approx Time: 4-6 hours.
Route: From the campsite follow the path which runs
beside the Allt Undalain. After a short distance cross
the bridge over the river and continue on the path S and
then W round the flanks of Sgurr Mhic Bharraich. Still
on the path climb as far as Loch Coire nan Crogachan
from where you should climb steep heathery slopes N
to gain the E ridge near the summit. Once on the ridge
the summit is a short distance to the NW. Return to
Gleann Undalain by the broad E ridge.
Stalking Information: Glenshiel and Cluanie Estates.
Tel: 059981-282.

Mountain: Am Bathach, 2618ft/798m.
Map: OS Sheet 33: GR 073144.
Translation: the byre.
Pronunciation: *am baa-hoch*.
Access Point: A87, 1 ml E of Cluanie Inn.
Distance/ascent: 4mls/2000ft; 6km/610m.
Approx Time: 3-4 hours.
Route: Just W of the Allt a'Chaorainn Mhoir a gate gives access to an old stalker's path which runs alongside a forestry plantation. Beyond the plantation and the fizzled out path, follow the ridge in a NW direction to the first top at 730m. From there continue along the grassy ridge to the summit.
Stalking Information: Corrielair Estate.
Tel: 0320-40237/40246.

Mountain: Sgurr an Airgid, 2759ft/841m.
Map: OS Sheet 33; GR 940227.
Translation: peak of silver.
Pronunciation: *skoor an er-e-kit*.
Access Point: Ruarach, Strath Croe, GR 960217.
Distance/ascent: 4mls/2700ft; 6km/823m.
Approx Time: 4-5 hours.
Route: From Strath Croe follow the stalker's path beside the burn, then follow it as it traverses the hillside in a W direction. Continue on the path as it turns back on itself and climbs to the bealach to the E of Sgurr an Airgid. Climb W up the undulating and rocky ridge to the summit. Return the same way.
Stalking Information: Mr R Carr, Inverinate Estate, Kyle, Wester Ross. Ex-directory telephone number, so write for permission.

25 Glen Affric to Strathfarrar

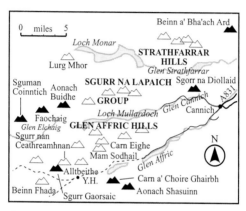

Suggested Base Accommodation	Shiel Bridge or Cannich. Hotels, guest houses and b&b in Shiel Bridge, Dornie, Kyle of Lochalsh, and Cannich. Youth hostels at Ratagan, Cannich and Alltbeith. Camping/caravan sites at Beauly, Muir of Ord and Drumnadrochit.
Public Transport	Rail: Inverness to Wick and Thurso, and Inverness to Kyle of Lochalsh. Station at Muir of Ord for onward post bus service. Buses: Inverness to Dingwall, Tain and Dornoch. Inverness to Garve and Ullapool for Beauly and Muir of Ord for onward post bus service. Post Buses: Beauly to Tomich for Struy and Cannich. Muir of Ord to Strathconon for Inverchoran.

Mountain: Carn a'Choire Ghairbh, 2837ft/865m
           Aonach Shasuinn, 2917ft/889m.
Map: OS Sheets 25/34; GR 137189, GR 173180.
Translation: cairn of the rough corrie, height of the sassenach.
Pronunciation: *kaarn a chora char-av, oenach has-yin.*
Access Point: Forestry Commission car park, E of Affric Lodge.
Distance/ascent: 16mls/3800ft; 26km/1158m.
Approx Time: 7-10 hours.
Route: Leave the car park and follow the forestry road W through the Pollan Buidhe forest on the S side of Loch Affric. Pass a white cottage, and continue to the Allt Garbh. A footpath follows the W bank of the burn, but after a short distance bear away to the W and climb the steep slopes of Na Cnapain. Continue WSW to Carn Glas Iochdarach, down to a col on the broad ridge and then continue on the ridge to the summit of Carn a'Choire Ghairbh. To reach Aonach Shasuinn, descend SSW down steep slopes to a broad col and the headweaters of the Allt Garbh. Climb the N slopes of Carn a'Coire Ghuirm and continue to Loch a'Choinich. From the loch head NE along the ridge of An Elric and down to another col at the foot of Aonach Shasuinn's W ridge. Follow this ridge to the west top and finally walk ESE to the summit. To descend, return to the W summit and descend the N ridge to Loch an Sguid. From there follow the stalker's path on the N bank of the Allt Garbh back to the forestry road.
Stalking Information: Forestry Commission.
Tel: 0320-6322.

Mountain: Sgurr Gaorsaic, 2752ft/839m.
Map: OS Sheet 33: GR 036218.
Translation: peak of thrills.
Pronunciation: *skoor gower-sak.*
Access Point: Dorusduain, Strath Croe.
Distance/ascent: 9mls/3200ft; 14km/975m.
Approx Time: 6-8 hours.

Route: From Dorusduain, cross the footbridge to the S bank of the river in Gleann Choinneachain and follow this path SE up the glen. This path eventually leads to the Bealach an Sgairne - go through the pass and drop down to the S end of Loch a'Bhealaich. Once you pass the loch, leave the path and climb the SW slopes of Sgurr Gaorsaic to the level summit. Return the same way.
Stalking Information: National Trust for Scotland.
Tel: 059981-219.

Mountain: Sguman Coinntich, 2883ft/879m
Faochaig, 2847ft/868m.
Map: OS Sheet 25: GR 977304, GR 022317.
Translation: mossy peak, the whelk.
Pronunciation: *skoo-man chon-yeech, fouch-ag.*
Access Point: Killilan, Loch Long.
Distance/ascent: 15mls/4100ft; 25km/1250m.
Approx Time: 7-10 hours.
Route: Leave Killilan and take the path which runs E up the N bank of the Allt a'Choire Mhoir. As the angle of the climb eases climb SE up the slopes of the Sguman Coinntich ridge. Gain the ridge and continue in a ENE direction to the summit. To reach Faochaig, continue in a NE direction to overlook the Bealach Mhic Bheathain and then change direction to descend the E ridge to bumpy ground S of Sron na Gaoithe. Climb to this summit and follow the ridge E around the head of Coire Searrach to the S slopes of Faochaig. Climb these slopes to the summit. Descend S into Coire Domhain where a stalker's path on the E bank of the burn leads to Carnach in upper Glen Elchaig. Return to Killilan by the long walk down Glen Elchaig.
Stalking Information: Killilan Estate.
Tel: 059988-262.

Mountain: Aonach Buidhe, 2949ft/899m.
Map: OS Sheet 25: GR 058324.
Translation: yellow ridge.
Pronunciation: *oenach boo-ee.*
Access Point: Iron Bridge, GR 043295.

Distance/ascent: 5mls/2500ft; 8km/762m (from Iron Bridge).

Approx Time: 4-5 hours.

Route: This Corbett is perhaps best climbed in association with Faochaig, but such an expedition would probably require an overnight camp. Alternatively, a mountain bike up the length of Glen Elchaig from Killilan is strongly recommended. From Iron Lodge, (8mls/13km from Killilan) follow the track up the N side of the Allt na Doire Ghairbh, taking the right hand branch of the track where it splits. Cross the An Cromallt and immediately leave the path to follow the S ridge, steeply at first, then easily all the way to the summit. An alternative descent is by way of the superb NE ridge, returning to Iron Lodge by way of the pass which contains Loch Mhoicean.

Stalking Information: Killilan Estate.

Tel: 059988-262.

Mountain: Sgorr na Diollaid, 2684ft/818m.

Map: OS Sheet 25: GR 282362.

Translation: peak of the saddle.

Pronunciation: *skoor na jeel-at.*

Access Point: Muchrachd, Glen Cannich, GR 287338.

Distance/ascent: 4mls/2100ft; 6km/640m.

Approx Time: 3-4 hours.

Route: Take the minor road from Glen Cannich towards Muchrachd but before the road bends to the right take to the hillside left of the forest plantation. Take a straight line due N to the summit. Return the same way.

Stalking Information: Forestry Commission.

Tel: 0320-6322.

Mountain: Beinn a'Bha'ach Ard, 2827ft/862m.

Map: OS Sheet 26: GR 361435.

Translation: hill of the high byre.

Pronunciation: *byn a vach-art.*

Access Point: Inchmore, Glen Strathfarrar.

Distance/ascent: 9mls/2600ft; 14km/792m.

Approx Time: 6-8 hours.

Route: Walk up the glen from the locked gate at Inchmore to the Power Station at Culligran. A track leaves the road here in a WSW direction through birch woods and along the N bank of the Neaty Burn. The path stops at a small dam, but continue up the E bank of the burn until you reach the Allt Doire Bhuig. Follow this stream in a NE direction all the way to the summit.

Stalking Information: Culligran Estate.
Tel: 0463-76285.

26 Achnashellach, Torridon and Applecross

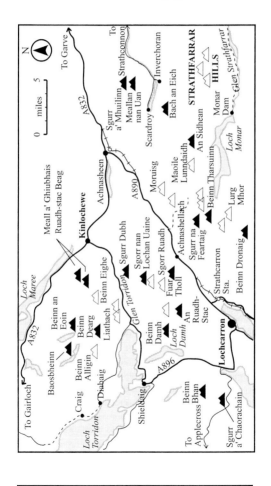

Suggested Base	Lochcarron.
Accommodation	Hotels, guest houses and b&b at Achnasheen, Strathcarron and Torridon. Youth hostel at Torridon. Private hostel at Craig, Achnashellach.
Public Transport	Rail: Inverness to Kyle of Lochalsh. Stations at Achnasheen, Achnashellach and Strathcarron. Buses: Inverness to Poolewe for Achnasheen and Kinlochewe for onward post bus service. Post Buses: Achnasheen to Laide for Kinlochewe; Kinlochewe to Diabeg for Torridon.

Mountain: Meallan nan Uan, 2755ft/840m
          Sgurr a'Mhuilinn, 2884ft/879m.
Map: OS Sheet 25: GR 264545, GR 265558.
Translation: little hill of the lambs, peak of the mill.
Pronunciation: myalan nan oo-an, skoor a voo-lin.
Access Point: Strathanmore, GR 295546.
Distance/ascent: 5mls/3200ft; 8km/975m.
Approx Time: 4-6 hours.
Route: Follow the S bank of the Allt an t-Strathain Mhoir up a steep bank until you reach the 400m contour. Leave the stream now and walk in a SW direction up steep slopes to the obvious top called Creag Ruadh. From here descend in a NW direction into the first of two dips, and follow the ridge in a NW direction to Meallan nan Uan, climbing steeper slopes to gain the summit. Continue in a NW direction around the head of Coire a'Mhuillin, crossing an obvious knoll to a bealach. Climb the slopes to the NNE to gain the Sgurr a'Mhuillin ridge. The summit trig point is at the E end of the ridge. Descend by way of the ESE ridge and as it begins to level out into a flatter boggy area, cross the burn and descend back to Strathanmore on the S bank of the stream.
Stalking Information: Strathconon Estate.
Tel: 09977-207.

Mountain: Bac an Eich, 2787ft/849m.
Map: OS Sheet 25: GR 222489.
Translation: bank of the horse.
Pronunciation: bachk an ech .
Access Point: Inverchoran, GR 262503.
Distance/ascent: 6mls/2300ft; 10km/701m.
Approx Time: 4-6 hours.
Route: Take the Land Rover track which runs S from
the farm. This track rises steeply into Gleann Chorainn
for just over a mile. From the end of the track a footpath drops down to the burn and crosses it just beyond
the edge of the forest. Continue on this footpath down
Gleann Chorainn for just over half a mile or so then
leave it, bearing W to climb the broad shoulder which
leads into Coire an Lochain. Continue climbing this
shoulder, with the Loch Toll Lochain below you on your
right, over some steep and rocky ground until you reach
the more level summit ridge. Follow this ridge over wet
and boggy ground to the final rise to the summit. Either
return the same way, or alternatively, continue over Bac
an Eich in a NW direction, dropping steeply down to
Corriefeol from where a good footpath will bring you
pleasantly back to Inverchoran by way of Loch
Beannacharain.
Stalking Information: Strathconon Estate.
Tel: 09977-207.

Mountain: An Sidhean, 2670ft/814m.
Map: OS Sheet 25: GR 171454.
Translation: the fairy hill.
Pronunciation: an shee-an.
Access Point: Loch Monar Dam, GR 202395.
Distance/ascent: 10mls/2000ft; 16km/610m.
Approx Time: 4-7 hours.
Route: From the dam follow the road N as far as Monar
Lodge. From there a superb stalker's path follows the
N shore of Loch Monar. Disregard the first bifurcation
of tracks, continuing on the main track and at the sec-
ond junction take the path which runs N for a short
distance beside the Allt na Cois. Follow this path up,
and across the hill, as it begins to swing back on itself

leave it for the open hill heading N up the Mullach a'Gharbh-leathaid. After an initial steep ascent the ridge begins to level out into a wide plateau. Continue N to the summit cairn.

Stalking Information: Monar Estates.
Tel: 046376-267.

<hr>

Mountain: Beinn Tharsuinn, 2830ft/863m
　　　　　　Sgurr na Feartaig, 2827ft/862m.
Map: OS Sheet 25: GR 055433, GR 055454.
Translation: transverse hill, peak of the thrift.
Pronunciation: *byn tar-syn, skoor na feer-tag.*
Access Point: Craig, Glen Carron.
Distance/ascent: 10mls/3500ft; 16km/1067m.
Approx Time: 5-8 hours.
Route: A forestry road leaves the A890 just E of Gerry's Hostel at Craig. Follow this road through the forest and onto the open ground beyond, following the course of the Allt a'Chonais. Continue on the track until it begins to bear E by way of Pollan Buidhe. There is an old footbridge crossing the river here, which gives access to the Bealach Bhearnais footpath. Climb to the summit of the pass, leave the path and climb steeply in a SW direction to gain the broad grassy ridge which leads to the summit of Beinn Tharsuinn. (The vast majority of Munroists will have already climbed the Corbett as it is en route to Bidein a'Choire Sheasgaich and Lurg Mhor.) Return to the Bealach Bernais and climb steep slopes in a NW direction to the rocky summit of Sgurr na Feartaig. Return to the Allt a'Chonais track by way of the stalker's path which runs N then NNE from the summit.

Stalking Information: Achnashellach Estate.
Tel: 05206-266.

<hr>

Mountain: Beinn Dronaig, 2615ft/797m.
Map: OS Sheet 25: GR 037382.
Translation: hill of the knoll.
Pronunciation: *byn dron-ack.*
Access Point: Attadale, A890, GR 924391.

Fuar Tholl from Beinn Liath Mor

Distance/ascent: 19mls/30km from Attadale and back. 4mls/1750ft; 6km/533m from Bendronaig Lodge to the summit and back to the Lodge.

Approx Time: From Bendronaig Lodge, 2-4 hours.

Route: A mountain bike is highly recommended for the very long walk-in to this very remote hill. Follow the Land Rover track from Attadale House all the way to Bendronaig Lodge. The Corbett is then climbed by way of the steep slopes SE of the lodge. Climb these slopes to gain the summit ridge which is then followed in a ENE direction, over several bumps, to the trig point.

Stalking Information: Attadale Estate.

Tel: 05202-308.

Mountain: Fuar Tholl, 2976ft/907m.

Map: OS Sheet 25: GR 975489.

Translation: cold hole.

Pronunciation: *foo-ur howl.*

Access Point: Achnashellach Station.

Distance/ascent: 8mls/2900ft; 13km/884m.

Approx Time: 5-7 hours.

Route: From the station cross the railway line and into the forest. At the first junction in the forestry road turn left and follow this road for just over a quarter of a mile to where a small cairn beside a stream indicates a footpath to the left. This path soon joins the stalker's path which runs alongside the River Lair into Coire Lair. As the corrie opens out in front of you at the 400m contour, the path divides. Go W, crossing the river, and climb for about 250m before turning S into Coire Mainnrichean towards the foot of the impressive Mainreachan Buttress. Climb steeply up the corrie slopes, with the Buttress on your right, to reach a shallow col on the summit ridge. The trig point is now only a few metres to the NE. Descend W around the head of the Mainreachan Buttress and down steep rocky slopes to the broad col between Fuar Tholl and the Munro, Sgorr Ruadh. Find the path which runs E back to Coire Lair and descend back to the river.

Stalking Information: Achnashellach Estate.
Tel: 05206-266.

Mountain: An Ruadh-stac, 2926ft/892m.
Map: OS Sheet 25: GR 922481.
Translation: the red conical hill.
Pronunciation: *an roo-ugh stachk.*
Access Point: A890 at Coulags.
Distance/ascent: 9mls/2900ft; 14km/884m.
Approx Time: 5-8 hours.
Route: Park near the disused gravel pit at Coulags bridge on the S side off the A890. Cross the road and follow the track beside the Fionn-abhainn towards Coire Fionnarach. Continue on this track, past the bothy and the Stone of Fingal's Dog, the Clach nan Con-fionn. Shortly after the stone the path divides. Take the left fork and climb up below Meall nan Ceapairean to the

An Ruadh-stac and the Munro Maol Chean-dearg

Bealach a'Choire Ghairbh between Ceapairean, the Munro Maol Chean-dearg in the N and An Ruadh-stac in the W. Leave the bealach in a S direction then follow a rough ridge SW between two lochans to the final slopes of the mountain. These slopes are rough with a fair bit of scrambling involved to reach the summit. The S summit is the higher.

Stalking Information: Achnashellach Estate.
Tel: 05206-266.

Mountain: Sgurr a'Chaorachain, 2598ft/792m.
Map: OS Sheet 24: GR 797417.
Translation: peak of the little field of berries.
Pronunciation: *skoor a choe-rach-yin.*
Access Point: Bealach na Ba road at a bridge, GR 814413.
Distance/ascent: 5mls/2300ft; 8km/701m.
Approx Time: 3-5 hours.
Route: Follow the path up the E side of the burn and along the E shore of Loch Coire nan Arr to the head of the loch. Leave the loch and climb due W with the great prow of A'Chioch on your right. Climb the slopes into the corrie. High up in the corrie there is a small lochan, backed by a very steep sandstone cliff. Just S of the cliff a very steep grassy slope leads to a col on the summit ridge. The summit is about half a mile along the ridge to the E. Return to your starting point either by following the ridge W to the summit of the Bealach na Ba road, and then back down the road, or alternatively, continue ESE from the summit along the ridge. This becomes rather tricky in places and some scrambling is required but stick with a bearing of SE as it steepens and you should avoid the major difficulties.

Stalking Information: Applecross Estate.
Tel: 05203-249.

Mountain: Beinn Bhan, 2939ft/896m.
Map: OS Sheet 24: GR 804450.
Translation: white hill.
Pronunciation: *byn vaan.*
Access Point: Bridge over River Kishorn, GR 834423.

Distance/ascent: 8mls/3000ft; 13km/914m.
Approx Time: 5-8 hours.
Route: Follow the path from the bridge N for 1½mls/ 2.4km before leaving it to climb the slopes which lead to Lochan Coire na Poite. From here there is a choice of routes to the summit. Scramblers will opt for the tight ridge of A'Chioch, the crest of which becomes narrow before dropping to cross an intermediate top before a steep rocky climb presents itself as a barrier to the summit plateau. There are, however, traces of a path up this steep section and although exposed, there are no real difficulties for the experienced scrambler. Those who would rather refrain from using their hands can gain the summit plateau by the ridge which forms the N side of Coire na Fhamhair, N of the Lochan Coire a'Poite. This route only some very mild scrambling. Descend from the summit by following the narrowing plateau in a SE direction to the head of Loch Kishorn.
Stalking Information: Applecross Estate.
Tel: 05203-249.

Mountain: Beinn Damh, 2959ft/902m.
Map: OS Sheet 24: GR 893502.
Translation: hill of the stag.
Pronunciation: byn dav.
Access Point: A896, Loch Torridon Hotel.
Distance/ascent: 7mls/2900ft; 11km/884m.
Approx Time: 5-7 hours.

Beinn Damh in Torridon

Sgorr nan Lochan Uaine from Beinn Liath Mor

Route: About 100m W of a bridge over the Allt Coire Roill a stalker's path runs S through some woodland beside the gorge through which the river flows. Beyond a prominent waterfall the forest begins to thin out and the path divides. Go right and follow this path in a SW direction into the Toll Ban corrie. Climb the steep upper slopes to gain the col between Sgurr na Bana Mhoraire and Beinn Damh. Climb the slopes in a SE direction to the first of the false summits which can be bypassed on the right. Cross a boulder-strewn dip to the next summit from where a narrowing ridge leads to the true summit.
Stalking Information: Ben Damh Estate.
Tel: 044587-252.

Mountain: Sgorr nan Lochan Uaine, 2863ft/873m
              Sgurr Dubh, 2566ft/782m.
Map: OS Sheet 25: GR 969532, GR 979558.
Translation: peak of the green lochan, black peak.
Pronunciation: *skoor nan loch-an wayne, skoor doo*.
Access Point: Car Park on A896 road in Glen Torridon at foot of Coire Dubh.
Distance/ascent: 8mls/2600ft; 13km/792m.
Approx Time: 5-8 hours.
Route: About 100m E of the car park a footpath leaves the S side of the road and passes the Ling Hut as it runs SW close to the Allt Frianach before entering the corrie of a thousand knolls, Coire a'Cheud-chnoic. The path

threads its way S through these hillocks and continues S until below the col between Sgorr nan Lochan Uaine and Beinn Liath Mor. Climb SE up the heather-clad slopes to the lochan itself. From here a steep scramble in a NE direction leads to the summit. Continue past the summit in a NNE direction and follow the broad humpy ridge downhill to a broad col with a scattering of lochans. Continue in a NNE direction to the summit of Sgurr Dubh. Return to the lochan-splattered col, and descend directly to the W to return to the stalker's path. *Stalking Information:* Coulin Estate. *Tel:* 044584-244.

Mountain: Ruadh-stac Beag, 2940ft/896m
Meall a'Ghiubhais, 2910ft/887m.
Map: OS Sheet 19: GR 973614, GR 976634.
Translation: small red conical hill, hill of the fir tree.
Pronunciation: *roo-ugh stachk bayk, myowl a choo-vash.*
Access Point: Aultroy Visitor Centre, A832 at Anancaun.
Distance/ascent: 11mls/4300ft; 18km/1311m.
Approx Time: 6-9 hours.
Route: Climb the old pony track which runs W from the Visitor Centre. At the end of the track, on the 400m contour, bear N to follow a stream up to the final bouldery slopes of Meall a'Ghiubhais. Climb these slopes to the summit plateau. The summit is at the SW end of this plateau. Return to the track and continue past it in a SE direction to pick up the line of the Allt Toll a'Ghiubhais. Follow this stream up into the high bealach between Ruadh-stac Beag and the main ridge of Beinn Eighe and then climb the Corbett by its loose scree covered S slopes. Return the way you came to the Pony Track.
Stalking Information: Scottish Natural Heritage. Access via the pony track to these two Corbetts is unrestricted throughout the year.

Mountain: Beinn Dearg, 2998ft/914m.
Map: OS Sheet 19, 24 & 25: GR 895608.
Translation: red hill.
Pronunciation: *byn jerrack.*
Access Point: Coire Mhic Nobuil car park, GR 869576.
Distance/ascent: 9mls/3600ft; 14km/1097m.
Approx Time: 6-9 hours.
Route: Follow the footpath up Coire Mhic Nobuil and after crossing the footbridge over the Abhainn Coire Mhic Nobuil take the footpath that branches off to the left towards the Horns of Alligin. Follow this path almost as far as the Bealach a'Chomla between Aligin and Beinn Dearg and bear off to the right to climb the steep and craggy W spur of Stuc na Cabhaig. From here a tight rocky ridge leads to the flat summit of Beinn Dearg. To descend, traverse the mountain in a SE direction down an easy ridge. After a short distance the ridge turns to the E and a short but steep descent leads to a col. Cross it and follow the ridge again as it rises and becomes tight and rocky, giving some fairly exposed scrambling. The E ridge is reached by a couple of short rocky steps and the going becomes easier all the way to Carn na Feola. Descend the slopes to the S to regain the Coire Mhic Nobuil path. The S side of Beinn Dearg's E ridge is very steep and precipitous in places. Walkers are advised to continue on the E ridge as far as Carn na Feola.
Stalking Information: National Trust for Scotland. No restrictions.

Mountain: Baosbheinn, 2871ft/875m.
            Beinn an Eoin, 2805ft/855m.
Map: OS Sheet 19: GR 871654, GR 905646.
Translation: wizard's hill, hill of the bird.
Pronunciation: *boe-shvyn, byn an yaween.*
Access Point: A832, GR 857721.
Distance/ascent: 13mls/4900ft; 21km/1494m.
Approx Time: 7-10 hours.
Route: Start at the old shed known as the Red Barn on the A832. Cross the footbridge on the S side of the road and follow the track SE for 3mls/5km to a stream cross-

ing just before Loch na h-Oidhche. Once across the stream leave the path and strike uphill in a SW direction to gain the main Beinn an Eoin ridge. This undulates over several tops before its final narrow section which leads to the trig point summit. Descend steep slopes to the S to reach Gorm Loch na Beinne. From here cross the flat wet ground W to reach the S end of the Baosbheinn ridge. Climb the broad ridge, over two subsidiary summits to the final steep pull to the main top, Sgorr Dubh. Traverse the mountain as far N as Creag an Fhithich and descend the NE slopes of the hill, bearing as far to the right as you can to reach the moorland. Continue N, as you may experience difficulty in crossing the Abhainn a'Garbh Choire to the path on its E bank, to Loch Bad an Sgalaig, crossing the stream by the footbridge and following the E shores back to the A832.

Stalking Information: Gairloch Estate.
Tel: 0445-2374.

27 Dundonnell and Fisherfield

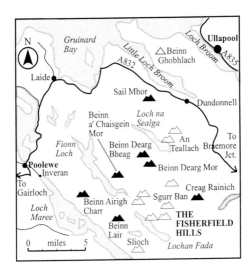

Suggested Base Accommodation	Kinlochewe or Dundonnell. Hotels, b&b in Kinlochewe, Poolewe. Private hostel at Sail Mhor, Dundonnell. Caravan site at Kinlochewe. Camping/caravan site at Gairloch.
Public Transport	Rail: Inverness to Kyle of Lochalsh, nearest station at Garve and Achnasheen for onward bus services. Buses: Inverness to Poolewe for Kinlochewe. Inverness to Braemore and Gairloch for Dundonnell.

████████████

Mountain: Beinn Lair, 2821ft/860m.
Map: OS Sheet 19: GR 982732.
Translation: hill of the mare.
Pronunciation: *byn layer*.
Access Point: Poolewe.
Distance/ascent: From Kernsary, 16mls/3000ft; 26km/914m.
Approx Time: 8-10 hours.
Route: Walk, or preferably cycle, along the track on the E bank of the River Ewe as far as Kernsary. From here a track leads to a plantation where it forks. Take the right fork through the plantation. Where the track suddenly bends to the left carry straight on to exit the plantation beside the Allt na Creige. Continue on this very muddy and sometimes indistinct path, past Loch an Doire Crionaich to the foot of Strathan Buidhe. Cross the stream which issues from this narrow glen and pick up the footpath again on the E bank, turning round the N slopes of Meall Mheinnidh.

As the track comes closer to the S shore of Fionn Loch look out for another path coming in from the S. Take this path, climbing up to the top of the Bealach Mheinnidh. From the bealach ascend the slopes in a NE direction to gain the Beinn Lair ridge, a superb walk overlooking some of the wildest landscape in Scotland. Continue on the ridge in a SE direction to the large summit cairn. Return the way you came.
Stalking Information: Ardlair/Fisherfield/Letterewe Estates.
Tel: 044586-215.

████████████

Mountain: Beinn Airigh Charr, 2595ft/791m.
Map: OS Sheet 19: GR 930762.
Translation: hill of the rough shieling.
Pronunciation: *byn aaree chaar*.
Access Point: Poolewe.
Distance/ascent: From Kernsary, 10mls/2500ft; 16km/762m.
Approx Time: 5-7 hours.

Route: Walk or cycle along the track on the E bank of
the River Ewe as far as Kernsary. Take the path which
runs S towards Loch Maree. Just before you reach the
Ruidh Dorcha woods look out for a stone sheep fold on
your left. A path runs E from here joining a stream which
flows down from a bealach between Spidean nan Clach
and Meall Chnaimhean. From this bealach climb the
steep W slopes of Beinn Airigh Charr to its trig point
summit. Return the samw way.
Stalking Information: Ardlair/Fisherfield/Letterewe
Estates.
Tel: 044586-215.

Mountain: Beinn a'Chaisgein Mor, 2812ft/857m.
Map: OS Sheet 19: GR 983785.
Translation: big forbidding hill.
Pronunciation: *byn a chas-ken more.*
Access Point: Poolewe.
Distance/ascent: 24mls/3000ft; 38km/914m.
Approx Time: 10-12 hours.
Route: Follow the route for Beinn Lair as far as the
junction of the paths below the Bealach Mheinnidh.
From the junction cross N over the causeway between
the Fionn Loch and the Dubh Loch to Carnmore. Take
the stalker's path which traverses E just before
Carnmore, below the cliffs of Sgurr na Laocainn, then
NE beside the Allt Bruthach an Easain as far as Lochan
Feith Mhic'illean. From the lochan climb the broad E
shoulder of Beinn a'Chaisgein Mor to the summit. Re-
turn the same way.
Stalking Information: Ardlair/Fisherfield/Letterewe
Estates.
Tel: 044586-215.

Mountain: Creag Rainich, 2647ft/807m.
Map: OS Sheet 19/20: GR 096751.
Translation: bracken crag.
Pronunciation: *krayk ranyeech.*
Access Point: A832 at Loch a'Bhraoin.
Distance/ascent: 10mls/2000ft; 16km/610m.
Approx Time: 4-6 hours.

Route: Take the track from the road down to Loch a'Bhraoin. Follow the path which follows the N shore of the loch all the way to the cottage of Lochivraon. Climb the slopes behind the cottage on a long and relentless pull in a NW direction to an un-named outlier at 749m, then over a slight col to the summit beyond.
Stalking Information: Inverbroom Estate.
Tel: 085485-229.

Mountain: Beinn Dearg Mor, 2985ft/910m
Beinn Dearg Bheag, 2690ft/820m.
Map: OS Sheet 19: GR 032799, GR 020812.
Translation: big red hill, little red hill.
Pronunciation: *byn jerrack more, byn jerrack beyk.*
Access Point: A832 Car park at Corrie Hallie.
Distance/ascent: 16mls/4500ft; 26km/1371m.
Approx Time: 9-12 hours.
Route: S of the road, follow the track through Gleann Chaorachain and onto the high moorland W of Loch Coire Chaorachain. Soon, a path bears off to the right, skirting the foot of the Sail Liath ridge of An Teallach and dropping down to the bothy at Shenavall. From the bothy, cross the Abhainn Strath na Sealga, half a mile of wet and boggy moorland, and finally the Abhainn Gleann na Muice to reach Larachantivore. In spate conditions don't even attempt to ford these rivers which can become very high and fast in a surprisingly short time. From Larachantivore take the path S for a hundred yards or so then take to the hill, making a rising traverse towards Beinn Dearg Mor's SE corrie. From this corrie you can either ascend the narrow ridge on its SW side, or ascend the slopes up the middle of the corrie.

Descend in a SW direction, soon turning to a NW direction as you reach the ridge which leads to Beinn Dearg Bheag, rounding the head of Toll an Lochain. Follow the ridge to the summit. To descend, follow the ridge back to its low point above Toll an Lochain and follow the steep slopes on the NE side of this col, down to the footpath on the shore of Loch na Sealga and return to Corrie Hallie via Shenavall.
Stalking Information: Ardlair/Fisherfield/Letterewe Estates.
Tel: 044586-215.

Mountain: Sail Mhor, 2516ft/767m.
Map: OS Sheet 19: GR 033887.
Translation: big heel.
Pronunciation: *saal vore.*
Access Point: A835, Ardessie.
Distance/ascent: 6mls/2600ft; 10km/792m.
Approx Time: 4-6 hours.
Route: Pass the Ardessie Falls on the S south of the road and follow the path on the E bank of the Allt Airdeasaidh. At the point where the path peters out on the 300m contour, bear W to gain Sail Mhor's SE shoulder. Climb the shoulder N, then W to the summit. Descend by continuing round the summit crest, dropping down on the S ridge to the col between Sail Mhor and Ruigh Mheallain. From the col descend E to the Allt Airdeasaidh which can be followed back to the road.
Stalking Information: Dundonnell Estate.
Tel: 085483-219.

28 The Fannichs and Ullapool

Suggested Base	Garve or Ullapool.
Accommodation	Hotels, guest houses, b&b at Garve, Aultguish, Oykel Bridge and Ullapool. Youth hostel at Ullapool. Camping/caravan sites at Ullapool and Garve.
Public Transport	Rail: Inverness to Kyle of Lochalsh. Station at Garve for onward bus services. Buses: Inverness to Gairloch for Garve, Garbat, Aultguish, Dirrie More and Braemore. Inverness to Ullapool for Garve, Garbat, Aultguish, Dirrie Mor and Inverlael. Lairg to Lochinver for Oykel Bridge, (for Strath Mulzie).

Mountain: Little Wyvis, 2506ft/764m.
Map: OS Sheet 20: GR 430635.
Translation: little awesome hill.
Pronunciation: *little wee-vis.*
Access Point: A835, S of Garbat. GR 412673.
Distance/ascent: 6mls/1700ft; 10km/518m.
Approx Time: 4-6 hours.
Route: Take the muddy forestry path along the N bank of the Allt a'Bhealaich Mhoir in an E direction. Follow the path to the edge of the forest, then to a fence around more recent afforestation. Cross this fence by the stile provided, cross the stream and follow the fence S to the col between Tom na Caillich and Little Wyvis. From the col climb the summit slopes of Little Wyvis in a SSW direction — the summit is the southerly of the two tops.
Stalking Information: Forestry Commission.
Tel: 0349-62144.

Mountain: Beinn Liath Mhor a'Ghiubhais Li
         2513ft/766m.
Map: OS Sheet 20: GR 281713.
Translation: big grey hill of the coloured pines.
Pronunciation: *byn lyee-uy vore a yoo-ash lee.*
Access Point: A835, GR 278743.
Distance/ascent: 5mls/1700ft; 8km/518m.
Approx Time: 3-5 hours.
Route: Follow the rough path on the S bank of the Abhainn an Torrain Duibh for half a mile or so. Just where a tributary streams flows down from the N ridge of the Corbett to join it, leave the path and take to the N ridge, climbing S then SE over rough grass and heather slopes to the broad summit. Descend to the NE over Meall Daimh then N and NW back to the A835 road.
Stalking Information: Lochluichart Estate.
Tel: 0343-820213.

Mountain: Carn Chuinneag, 2749ft/838m.
Map: OS Sheet 20: GR 484833.
Translation: hill of the bucket.

Pronunciation: kaarn choonyak.
Access Point: Glencalvie Lodge, GR 466891.
Distance/ascent: 12mls/2500ft; 19km/762m.
Approx Time: 5-8 hours.
Route: The road which runs up Glen Calvie is private so cars should be left near the bridge. Follow the road which runs past the left side of the lodge, past a keeper's cottage. Continue S on the private road up Glen Calvie, past Diebidale Lodge (on the opposite side of the river) to a junction of paths. Ignore the one which leads off to the right, as this goes back to Diebidale Lodge. Take the stalker's path which runs S before zig-zagging up the N ridge of Carn Chuinneag. Follow this stalker's path to another junction of paths, (marked by a cairn). This time take the path to the left, following it for about half a mile to just below the col between the two tops. Leave the path and climb to the col from where it it an easy stroll to the E top and the trig point. Return the same way.
Stalking Information: Glencalvie Estate.
Tel: 08632-553.

Mountain: Beinn a'Chaisteil, 2581ft/787m.
Map: OS Sheet 20: GR 370801.
Translation: castle hill.
Pronunciation: byn a chash-tyal.
Access Point: A835 at Black Bridge, 1½mls/2.4km E of Aultguish Inn.
Distance/ascent: From Black Bridge, 13mls/2000ft; 21km/610m.
Approx Time: From Black Bridge, 6-8 hours. A mountain bike would save considerable time.
Route: The use of a mountain bike is strongly recommended for the approach to this hill. Follow the estate road N as far Lubriach. Shortly after here a rough track continues N beyond a locked gate, just before the road crosses to the W bank of the river. Follow the rough track past the forestry and then W to the shores of Loch Vaich. If you have used a mountain bike and intend returning over Meall a'Ghriannan, you may wish to leave it hereabouts to be collected on your return. An alternative is to continue by bike on the stony track N beside the loch to Lubach-laggan. From here, follow the burn

---

which flows down from Beinn a'Chaisteil making use
of the old disused stalker's path. Continue climbing in
a NE direction to the summit. Either descend the way
you came to Lubach-laggan, or continue S over Meall
a'Ghriannan to the rough track back to Lubriach and
Black Bridge.
Stalking Information: Strathvaich Estate.
Tel: 09975-230.

Mountain: Carn Ban, 2772ft/845m.
Map: OS Sheet 20: GR 238875.
Translation: white cairn.
Pronunciation: *kaarn baan.*
Access Point: A835 at Black Bridge, 1½mls/2.4km E
of Aultguish Inn.
Distance/ascent: Black Bridge to Gleann Beag: 10mls/
16km. Glean Beag to summit and back to Gleann Beag:
7mls/1650ft; 11km/503m.
Approx Time: From Gleann Beag to summit and back,
4-6 hours.
Route: The use of a mountain bike is strongly recommended for the approach to this hill as the first 10mls/
16km are all on tracks. Follow the route above for Beinn
a'Chaisteil as far as Lubach-laggan. Continue N to the
head of Loch Vaich, then N and NE to the col between
Beinn a'Chaisteil and Meall a'Chaorainn. Staying on
the track drop down around the E slopes of Meall
a'Chaorainn and then W into Gleann Beag. Cross the
river by the bridge and continue W almost as far as a
second bridge below the crags of Cail Mhor. A small
area of quarry workings gives access to a stalker's path
which diagonally ascends the hillside and climbs to Loch
Sruban Mora. From the E shore of the loch climb NE to
gain the long and undulating S ridge of Carn Ban, following it over improving terrain to the summit. Return
the same way.
Stalking Information: Deanich Estate.
Tel: 08632-553.

■■■■■■■■■■■■■■■

Mountain: Beinn Enaiglair, 2916ft/889m.
Map: OS Sheet 20: GR 225805.
Translation: hill of timid birds.
Pronunciation: *byn enak-lar*.
Access Point: A835, Braemore Junction.
Distance/ascent: 7mls/2300ft; 11km/701m.
Approx Time: 4-6 hours.
Route: A track runs through the forest from the N side of the A835. Follow this track in a NW direction for almost 1ml/1.6km to an old disused building. From there a stalker's path runs in a NE direction, out through the trees and past the Home Loch. Continue on this path as far as the bealach between Meall Doire Faid and Beinn Enaiglair, and from there climb the S slopes of Enaiglair to the grassy summit plateau. For an alternative return route, descend from the summit by way of the NW ridge to pick up another stalker's path which runs round the W side of the hill. Follow this path S to its junction with your original stalker's path which is then followed back past the Home Loch and into the forest.

Beinn Enaiglair can be combined in a longer expedition with Beinn Dearg, by continuing NE from the summit of Enaiglair to the high col below Iorguill. Cross this hill to pick up the W ridge of Beinn Dearg. Follow the ridge to the broad summit.
Stalking Information: Braemore Estate.
Tel: 085485-222.

29 Inverpolly, Assynt & the Far North

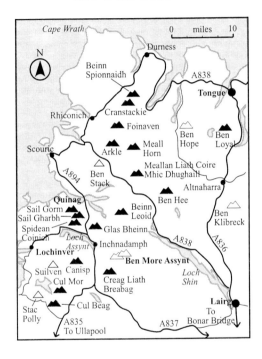

Cape Wrath

Durness

0   miles   10

N

Beinn
Spionnaidh

A838

Tongue

Rhiconich

Cranstackie

Foinaven

Ben
Hope

Ben
Loyal

Scourie

Arkle

Meall
Horn

Meallan Liath Coire
Mhic Dhughaill

Altnaharra

Ben
Stack

A894

Beinn
Leoid

Ben Hee

Ben
Klibreck

Quinag

Sail Gorm
Sail Gharbh

Spidean
Coinich

Glas Bheinn

Loch
Assynt

Inchnadamph

A838

A836

Lochinver

Ben More Assynt

Suilven

Canisp

Cul Mor

Creag Liath
Breabag

Loch
Shin

Lairg

Stac
Polly

Cul Beag

A835
To Ullapool

A837

To
Bonar Bridge

Suggested Base	Ullapool or Lairg.
Accommodation	Hotels, guest houses and b&b in Ullapool, Lairg, Inchnadamph, Kylesku, Scourie, Durness and Tongue. Youth hostels in Ullapool, Durness and Tongue. Camping/ caravan sites at Ullapool, Lairg, Durness and Tongue.

Public Transport   Rail: Inverness to Kyle of Loch-
alsh. Station at Garve for onward
bus services to Ullapool. (See Section 28). Inverness to Wick and
Thurso. Station at Lairg for onward post buses. Buses: Inverness
to Wick and Thurso for Bonar
Bridge; Inverness to Dornoch for
Bonar Bridge; Bonar Bridge to
Lairg; Lairg to Lochinver for
Inchnadamph; Thurso to Tongue.
Post Buses: Lairg to Talmine for
Crask Inn. Altnaharra to Port-
nacon and Rispond for Atna-
callich.

Mountain: Cul Beag, 2523ft/769m
Cul Mor, 2785ft/849m.
Map: OS Sheet 15: GR 140088, GR 162119.
Translation: small back, big back.
Pronunciation: *kool bayk, kool mo-ar.*
Access Point: A835, at Knockanrock, GR 188088.
Distance/ascent: 10mls/4500ft; 16kms/1371m.
Approx Time: 5-8 hours.

Cul Beag and Loch Lurgain

Cul Mor from Stac Pollaidh

Route: On the W side of the A835 just N of Knock-anrock a gate in the fence gives access to a boggy foot-path which goes N to gain the E ridge of Cul Mor. Fol-low this ridge to Meallan Diomhain, follow the ridge N to a small lochan in its shallow corrie, and from there continue W then SW up the steep and narrow ridge to the trig point summit. From the summit descend steeply W and then S to reach the high col between Cul Mor and Creag nan Calman.

From this col go E in a descending curve through to S and then SW to avoid the cliff above Lochan Dearg a'Chuil Mhoir. From the lochan make a descending traverse to the S to the outflow of Lochan Dearg, cross the burn and climb the slopes to the W to gain the promi-nent N ridge of Cul Beag. Follow the ridge to the sum-mit. Descend E to the high col between Cul Beag and Meall Dearg, cross Meall Dearg and follow the line of the Creag Dubh ridge E to pick up a stalker's path just S of Loch nan Ealachan. Follow this path to the A835 just S of Knockanrock.

Stalking Information: Glencanisp and Drumrunie Deer Forest Trust.

Tel: 05714-203.

Mountain: Creag Liath, Breabag, 2674ft/815m.
Map: OS Sheet 15: GR 287158.
Translation: grey crag, little height.
Pronunciation: *krayk lee-a, brae-bayk.*
Access Point: A837, GR 253178.
Distance/ascent: 6mls/2300ft; 10km/701m.
Approx Time: 4-6 hours.
Route: On the E side of the A837 where the Allt nan Uamh flows under the road there is a salmon hatchery. From here follow the burn E into its narrow glen to where it emerges from a spring in the river bed. Continue along the narrowing glen to a prominent cave entrance on the left. Leave the glen at this point, climbing steep slopes E and onto a more gently sloping hillside. Continue E, through an obvious breach in the escarpment and onto gentler slopes which lead to the broad summit ridge. Follow this ridge S to the 815m summit.
Stalking Information: Glencanisp and Drumrunie Deer Forest Trust.
Tel: 05714-203.

Mountain: Canisp, 2775ft/846m.
Map: OS Sheet 15: GR 203187.
Translation: white hill.
Pronunciation: *kaan-isp.*
Access Point: A837, GR 250159.
Distance/ascent: 7mls/2300ft; 11kms/701m.

Suilven (left) and Canisp

Approx Time: 4-6 hours.
Route: At the N end of Loch Awe a footbridge crosses the outflow and a wet path runs W to Loch na Gruagaich. Beyond the end of the path follow the line of the Allt Mhic Mhurchaidh Gheir and continue in a NW direction to gain the E ridge and Meall Diamhain. Descend to the slight col and continue W to gain the main summit ridge. Turn N and follow the ridge to the summit. Return the same way.
Stalking Information: Glencanisp and Drumrunie Deer Forest Trust.
Tel: 05714-203.

Mountain: Glas Bheinn, 2546ft/776m.
Map: OS Sheet 15: GR 255265.
Translation: grey hill.
Pronunciation: *ghlas-vyn.*
Access Point: A894, GR 238284.
Distance/ascent: 4mls/1800ft; 7km/549m.
Approx Time: 3-4 hours.
Route: From the road a footpath heads E to run round the S end of Loch na Gainmhich, but leave it before it reaches the loch to climb up the N slopes on the edge of the crags which line the NW ridge. Follow this ridge S then SE over several steps in the ridge to reach the broad, green summit plateau. Return the same way.
Stalking Information: Inchnadamph Estate.
Tel: 05712-221.

Mountain: Beinn Leoid, 2598ft/792m.
Map: OS Sheet 15: GR 320295.
Translation: sloping hill.
Pronunciation: *byn lee-ot.*
Access Point: A838, GR 357334.
Distance/ascent: 8mls/2500ft; 13km/762m.
Approx Time: 4-6 hours.
Route: Just over a mile S of Loch More there is a break in the forestry plantations, where a stalker's path climbs steadily S to reach a broad bealach between Meall na Leitreach and Meallan a'Chuail. From the bealach descend in a SW direction to pick up a stalker's path which

runs S to another high bealach above Loch Dubh. From here climb the E ridge directly to the summit. Return the same way.
Stalking Information: Kylestrome Estate.
Tel: 0971-2218.

Mountain: Quinag – Spidean Coinich, 2506ft/764m
          Sail Gharbh, 2651ft/808m
          Sail Gorm, 2546ft/776m
Map: OS Sheet 15: GR 205278, GR 209292, GR 198304.
Translation: milk bucket or water spout; mossy peak, rough heel, blue heel.
Pronunciation: *koon-yak, speet-yan kon-yeech, saal garv, saal gor-um.*
Access Point: A 894, GR 233274.
Distance/ascent: 9mls/3200ft; 14km/975m.
Approx Time: 5-8 hours.
Route: Leave the parking area beside the A894 and head due W to gain the prominent E ridge of Spidean Coinich. Follow this ridge to a rocky top which is crossed before a steep climb to the summit of Spidean. Head N to a high col and then over the bump marked on the map as 713m. Follow the path down to the Bealach a'Chornaidh. Continue N up steep slopes to Pt 745m then E along the narrowing ridge to the trig point on Sail Garbh. Return to the high col before Pt 745 and head NW across the latter's N slopes to gain the ridge which runs out to Sail Gorm. Return to Pt 745 and descend to the Bealach a'Chornaidh. From here a path runs down to the N shore of Lochan Bealach Cornaidh. This path soon joins up with a stalker's track which runs back to the starting point.
Stalking Information: Loch Assynt Estate.
Tel: 05712-216.

Mountain: Ben Hee, 2863ft/873m.
Map: OS Sheet 16: GR 426339.
Translation: fairly hill.
Pronunciation: *byn hee.*
Access Point: A838, West Merkland.

Distance/ascent: 7mls/2700ft; 11km/823m.
Approx Time: 4-6 hours.
Route: From the road take the private road N through a locked gate. Follow this road for almost a mile to where a small cairn marks a stalker's path leading off on the S bank of the Allt Coir a'Chruiteir. Follow this path up into a high corrie, bear SE to gain the broad SW shoulder and climb the boulder-strewn slopes to the summit. The summit itself is 20m beyond the trig point. Return the same way.
Stalking Information: Merkland Estate.
Tel: 054983-222.

Mountain: Meallan Liath Coire Mhic Dhughaill, 2628ft/801m.
Map: OS Sheets 15/16: GR 357392.
Translation: grey hill of MacDougall's corrie.
Pronunciation: myalan lee-ah corra vic doo-al.
Access Point: A838, Kinloch (S end of Loch More).
Distance/ascent: 10mls/2700ft; 16km/823m.
Approx Time: 5-8 hours.
Route: Follow the private estate road round the S shores of Loch More to the house at Aultanrynie. Just before you reach the house a stalker's path leads off in a NE direction. Folllow it, past a junction of paths and on up a series of zig zags to its termination point. From the end of the track head N up the broad and undulating ridge over Meallan Liath Beag to reach the Corbett's SE ridge just W of Carn Dearg. Follow this ridge W then NW and finally SW to the stony summit of Meallan Liath Coire Mhic Dughaill. Descend S, bearing slightly left to avoid the crags and descend over Meall Reinidh to rejoin the stalker's path. Return to Kinloch.
Stalking Information: Reay Forest.
Tel: 097184-221.

Mountain: Foinaven (Ganu Mor), 2989ft/911m
Arkle, 2581ft/787m
Meall Horn, 2550ft/777m.

Map: OS Sheet 9: GR 317507, GR 303462, GR 353449.

Translation: white hill (big wedge), hill of the level top, hill of the eagle.

Pronunciation: *foy-nayven, ar-kil, myowl horn.*

Access Point: Lone, GR 309422. This is the starting point for Meall Horn, Arkle and Foinaven. It is reached by a private road which leaves the A838 just N of Achfary. Permission to drive along this road to Lone is usually granted on enquiry to the estate office in Achfary.

Distance/ascent: 20½mls/6350ft; 32km/1935m.

Approx Time: 12-15 hours.

Route: Beyond the cottage at Lone a stalker's path follows the course of the Allt Horn, a stream which has its source in the communal bealach of these three Corbetts. To your left lie the slopes of Arkle, straight ahead the long gradient which leads to the Creag Dionard summit of Foinaven and to your right, the slopes of Meall Horn. You have a choice in which order you climb these hills, but since Foinaven is the biggest that's as good an arbiter as any. Continue up featureless slopes to Creag Dionard, the 778m un-named peak, where a broad rocky spur leads you on to the ridge itself. A few ups and downs, a lot of loose scree and much broken rock brings you to the highest point of Ganu Mor, where there are two cairns about a hundred metres apart.

Return the way you came back to the communal bealach. Climb the scrambly slopes of Creagan Meall Horn then across the saddle to the summit of Meall Horn. A direct bearing W will bring you back to the source of the Allt Horn and then up to Lochan na Faoileige, a superb high level lochan amid superb surroundings. Easy slopes then lead to the subsidiary top of Meall Aonghais, then a pull to Arkle's south top at 757m. From here a high level ridge walk of a mile or so takes you around the rim of Am Bathaaich, Arkle's east facing corrie, to the summit proper.

A return along the ridge to the south top, then a long descent west of Meall Aonghais drops you down to the stalker's path near your starting point at Lone.

Stalking Information: Reay Forest.
Tel: 097184-221.

Mountain: Cranstackie, 2624ft/800m
            Beinn Spionnaidh, 2532ft/772m.
Map: OS Sheet 9: GR 351556, GR 362573.
Translation: rugged hill, hill of strength.
Pronunciation: kraan-staky, byn spee-oan-ay.
Access Point: A838 at Carbreck, GR 333592.
Distance/ascent: 8mls/2500ft; 13km/762m.
Approx Time: 5-7 hours.
Route: Follow the private track S, over the River Dionard, as far as the shepherd's house at Rhigotter. From the house take to the open slopes to the SE to reach the high corrie and then the bealach between the two Corbetts. Climb Cranstackie directly by its well defined NE ridge then return to the col. Continue up the SW ridge of Beinn Spionnaidh to the trig point on the N end of the short summit ridge. Descend to Rhigotter by the WNW ridge.
Stalking Information: Balnakeil Estate.
Tel: 097181-268.

Mountain: Ben Loyal, 2506ft/764m.
Map: OS Sheet 10: GR 578489.
Translation: from Beinn Laghail, legal mountain.
Pronunciation: byn loy-al.
Access Point: Ribigill, GR 583538.
Distance/ascent: 9mls/2700ft; 14km/823m.
Approx Time: 5-8 hours.
Route: Drive to Ribigill on the minor road S from Tongue. A track runs due S from the farm to the old cottage at Cunside. From there continue S towards the rocky peak of Sgurr Chaonasaid, avoiding the rock by the grassy slopes to your left. From the summit the broad ridge continues due S to the main summit, An Caisteal, bypassing the rocks of Sgor a'Bhatain on the left. Climb the granite tor of An Caisteal from its W side. Complete the traverse of Ben Loyal by continuing S over a well defined ridge all the way to Carn an Tionail from where you should descend the grassy slopes to the W towards the Pt 568m.

Descend beside the Allt Fhionnaich to the 400m contour and then flank round the hill in a N direction until you can drop down to the woods of Coille na Cuile. Drop down through the woods and when clear of the trees return to Cunside below the NW slopes of the mountain.

Stalking Information: Ben Loyal Estate.
Tel: 084755-291/220.

30 The Islands

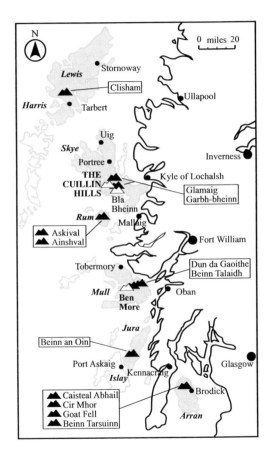

Arran

Suggested Base	Brodick.
Accommodation	Hotels, guest houses, b&b at Brodick and Lochranza. Youth hostel at Lochranza.
Public Transport	Ferry from Ardrossan to Brodick. Claonaig to Lochranza between April and October.

Mountain: Goatfell, 2867ft/874m.
Map: OS Sheet 69: GR 991415.
Translation: goat's hill.
Pronunciation: *as spelt.*
Access Point: Cladach near Brodick Castle.
Distance/ascent: 5mls/2950ft; 8km/899m.
Approx Time: 4-6 hours.
Route: A private road leads from Claddach, SW of Brodick Castle, and passes through the castle grounds. After half a mile or so the road ends and becomes a path which soon reaches the open hillside. The path continues and runs N up the slopes of Goatfell, skirting the obvious SE corrie to reach the prominent E ridge. Once on the ridge the path joins the track which runs up from Corrie. Scramble W along the ridge which is now quite steep in places, all the way to the summit trig point and direction indicator. Return the same way.
Stalking Information: National Trust for Scotland.
Tel: 0770-2202.

Mountain: Beinn Tarsuinn, 2710ft/826m
                Cir Mhor, 2621ft/799m
                Caisteal Abhail, 2818ft/859m.
Map: OS Sheet 69: GR 959412, GR 973432, GR 969444.
Translation: transverse hill, big comb, castle of the fork.
Pronunciation: *byn tarsh-yin, keer more, kashtyal aval.*
Access Point: Glen Rosa.

Distance/ascent: 13 mls/4600ft; 21km/1402m.

Approx Time: 6-8 hours.

Route: Follow the road from Brodick past Glenrosa Farm for just over a mile until you reach the path which runs W towards the Garbh Allt. Continue on this muddy path, crossing the burn at a small reservoir to the N bank. After a short distance the path leaves the Garbh Allt and heads NW towards Coire a'Bhradain. A cairn marks the path which leads on to the SE ridge of Beinn Nuis.

Follow the zig zags upwards to the summit. From Beinn Nuis the path continues N along the ridge to Beinn Tarsuinn. Continue over rough ground to the descent to the Bealach an Fhir-bhogha, where the path then divides. The lower path descends on the W side of the A'Chir ridge and traverses N to regain the ridge at the bealach between A'Chir and Cir Mhor. The higher path follows the line of the A'Chir ridge itself, a route which offers much exposed scrambling and some mild rock climbing sections. From the bealach, follow the straightforward SW ridge of Cir Mhor to the summit. Continue in a NW direction along the Hunter's Ridge to Caisteal Abhail. The summit is the second granite tor reached from the S. Follow the E ridge of Caisteal Abhail to the narrow gap below Ceum na Caillich.

Rather than climb the steep rocks head on, descend the obvious gully on the N side of the gap to a path on the right. This path soon rejoins the ridge beyond the summit rocks. Continue NE along the broad ridge to Suidhe Fhearghas. Just beyond this point a path zig zags down the slopes to the N into North Glen Sannox. Follow this path to its junction with another path which runs W from Sannox. From Sannox a bus will take you back to Brodick. It's best to check the bus times before leaving Brodick to save yourself a 7mls/11km road walk.

Stalking Information: National Trust for Scotland.

Tel: 0770-2202.

Jura

Suggested Base	Craighouse.
Accommodation	Hotels at Port Askaig, Islay and Craighouse, Jura. Guest houses and b&b at Port Askaig and at Feolin and Craighouse on Jura.
Public Transport	Ferry from Kennacraig to Port Askaig. A mountain bike would be very useful for getting around Jura.

Mountain: Beinn an Oir, 2578ft/786m.
Map: OS Sheet 61: GR 498749.
Translation: hill of gold.
Pronunciation: *byn an or*.
Access Point: A846, GR 543720.
Distance/ascent: 7mls/2500ft; 11km/762m.
Approx Time: 4-7 hours.
Route: Leave the road near the bridge over the Corran River and head in a NW direction over an obvious shoulder to reach the Corran River itself. Follow the river past Loch an t-Siob to reach the SE slopes of Beinn an Oir. A prominent grassy rake traverses across the E face of the hill in a S to N direction and this route allows much of the rough ground to be avoided. You soon reach the NE ridge and the final climb along a stone pathway to the summit.

Beinn an Oir can be climbed along with the other paps by tackling Beinn Shiantaidh by its SE shoulder from Loch an t-Siob. Descend by the W ridge to a col where Beinn an Oir can be climbed before descending the S ridge to reach Beinn a'Chaolais. Descend this latter top in an E direction to a col then NE to Glenn an t-Siob.
Stalking Information: Forest Estate.
Tel: 049-682230

Mull

Suggested Base	Craignure.
Accommodation	Hotels, guest houses and b&b at Craignure. Camp site at Craignure. Youth hostel at Tobermory.
Public Transport	Ferry from Oban to Craignure, or Lochaline to Fishnish. There is a regular bus service from Craignure to Bunessan and Fionnphort.

Mountain: Dun da Ghaoithe, 2512ft/766m.
Map: OS Sheet 49: GR 673362.
Translation: fort of the two winds.
Pronunciation: doon da goo-ee.
Access Point: Craignure.
Distance/ascent: 8mls/2500ft; 13km/762m.
Approx Time: 5-7 hours.
Route: Follow the A849 NW from Craignure for just over a mile to a bridge over the Scallastle River. Climb the easy open slopes to the SW on the N bank of the Allt an Dubh-Choire. Follow the broad ridge of Beinn Chreagach, bearing S to reach the summit of Dun da Ghaoithe. Descend by following the S ridge to Mainnir nam Fiadh and then E to the Telecom mast on Maol nan Uan. An access bulldozed track runs from there down to the A849 just S of Criagnure.
Stalking Information: Torosay Estate.
Tel: 06802-421.

Mountain: Beinn Talaidh, 2500ft/762m.
Map: OS Sheet 49: GR 625347.
Translation: hill of happiness (or hill of good pastures).
Pronunciation: byn tal-la.
Access Point: A849 at Glen Forsa, GR 643329.
Distance/ascent: 3mls/2100ft; 5km/640m.
Approx Time: 3-5 hours.

Route: Walk in a NW direction towards the broad shoulder of Maol nam Fiadh on Talaidh's S ridge. Once you gain the ridge follow it in a NNW direction to the summit. Return the same way.
Stalking Information: Glenforsa Estate.
Tel: 06803-424.

Rum

Suggested Base	Kinloch, Rum.
Accommodation	The Isle of Rum is a National Nature Reserve administered by Scottish Natural Heritage and permission must be sought from the Chief Warden before landing. Contact him at the White House, Isle of Rum, Inverness-shire. Tel: 0687-2026. There is a hotel at Kinloch Castle on the island, bunkhouse facilities and camping is usually allowed on the foreshore near the pier.
Public Transport	The Isle of Rum is reached by ferry from Mallaig (four days a week) or Arisaig.

Mountain: Askival, 2664ft/812m
　　　　　　Ainshval, 2563ft/781m.
Map: OS Sheet 39: GR 393952, GR 378944.
Translation: hill of ash trees, hill of strongholds.
Pronunciation: as-*ki-val, ayn-sh-val.*
Access Point: Kinloch.
Distance/ascent: Complete traverse of all the ridge, returning by the Dibidil footpath, 13mls/6000ft; 21km/1829m.
Approx Time: 8-12 hours.
Route: Head through the grounds of Kinloch Castle and take a well used path which runs in a SW direction beside the Allt Slugan a'Choilich towards Coire Dubh. From the headwaters of the stream in Corrie Dubh keep

Looking towards Hallival from the summit of Askival on the Isle of Rum

walking S to reach the gravelly Bealach Bairc-mheall. From the broad bealach go E then SE up the broad ridge of Hallival. Descend to the S, over a couple of awkward rocky steps to reach a narrow grassy ridge. Askival appears ahead as rocky and steep but is easily climbed until the Askival Pinnacle bars the way.

This steep rock can be climbed on its W side by a moderately difficult scramble, but can be avoided if necessary by a traverse on the E side of the ridge which leads, via some steep rocks, to the rocky summit. Descend W to the wide Bealach an Oir where you can either continue W to climb the fine peak of Trallval, or alternatively make a horizontal traverse below Trallval's E top to the Bealach an Fhuarain. From the bealach try and avoid the lower rocks of Ainshval's N ridge by traversing W to reach a prominent level stretch of ridge. From here follow the rocky ridge S to the summit. The narrow crest can be avoided by a narrow path on its E side which crosses some loose scree to reach the grassy summit.

The fifth of the Rum peaks is Sgurr nan Gillean, which can be reached easily from Ainshval by following the S ridge, over an intervening top to Gillean's long summit ridge. The summit is at the S end of the ridge. You can either return to Kinloch by traversing NW along the Leac a'Chaisteil and dropping N down into Glen Harris where a bulldozed track leads back to

Kinloch or alternatively, descend from Sgurr nan Gillean to Dibidil, where a footpath follows the coast back to Loch Scresort.

A third option, and slighty shorter than the other two, is to walk back the way you came to the Bealach an Oir, traverse the grassy slopes at the head of the Atlantic Corrie to the Bealach Bairc-mheall and back to Kinloch via Coire Dubh. The Dibidil path is probably the most popular route of return.

Stalking Information: Head Warden, Isle of Rum.

Tel: 0687-2026. The Isle of Rum is largely used for the study of red deer and various areas will be out of bounds from time to time. The Head Warden will advise you on your initial enquiry.

Skye

Suggested Base	Sligachan.
Accommodation	Hotels, guest houses, b&b at Broadford, Portree, Sligachan and Carbost. Youth hostels at Broadford and Glen Brittle. Camp site at Sligachan.
Public Transport	Rail: Inverness to Kyle of Lochalsh and Glasgow to Mallaig for ongoing ferries and bus service. Buses: Glasgow and Fort William to Uig. Ediinburgh and Perth to Portree. Inverness to Portree. Portree to Fiskavaig for Sligachan and Carbost. Post Bus: Broadford to Elgol for Loch Slapin.

Mountain: Glamaig, 2542ft/775m.
Map: OS Sheet 32: GR 514300.
Translation: greedy woman.
Pronunciation: *glaa-mig.*
Access Point: Sligachan.
Distance/ascent: 3mls/2500ft; 5km/762m.
Approx Time: 3-4 hours.

Route: Leave Sligachan and walk east along the A850 for a short distance before leaving the road and taking to the prominent W shoulder of the hill. Follow this shoulder and scree covered slopes to the summit. Traverse NE along the ridge to An Coileach. Descend from there in a NE direction then N to Sconser.
Stalking Information: Sconser Estate.
Tel: 047852-232.

Mountain: Garbh-bheinn, 2644ft/806m.
Map: OS Sheet 32: GR 531232.
Translation: rough hill.
Pronunciation: *garv-ven.*
Access Point: A850 at the head of Loch Ainort.
Distance/ascent: 5mls/3500ft; 8km/1067m.
Approx Time: 4-6 hours.
Route: Leave the road where it crosses the Abhainn Ceann Loch Ainort and head in a SW direction to gain the lower slopes of the Druim Eadar Da Choire. Follow this ridge to Pt 489m from where the ridge begins to narrow. Descend SE to a col then climb SSE on a increasingly rocky ridge to the summit of Garbh-bheinn. Descend NE down a fine ridge which gradually becomes wider and easier to the Bealach na Beiste. From the bealach climb the rocky and steep SW slopes of Belig to its summit. Descend the N ridge back to the starting point.
Stalking Information: Sconser Estate.
Tel: 047852-232.

Harris

Suggested Base	Tarbert.
Accommodation	Hotels, guest houses, b&b in Tarbert. Private hostel at Rhenigidale.
Public Transport	Ferry from Uig (Skye) to Tarbert, or Ullapool to Stornoway.

Mountain: Clisham, 2621ft/799m.
Map: OS Sheet 14: GR 155073.
Translation: rocky cliff.
Pronunciation: *klee-sham*.
Access Point: A859 at the bridge over the Maaruig River.
Distance/ascent: 4mls/2000ft; 6km/610m.
Approx Time: 3-4 hours.
Route: Leave the road and follow the slopes in a W direction to reach the shallow col to the N of the Sron Carsaclett. From here traverse the slopes in a NW direction to gain the broad S shoulder of the hill. Follow this shoulder to the SE ridge which is then followed to the narrow summit and trig point. Return the same way.

Further reading

Bennet, Donald (ed), *The Munros: the Scottish Mountaineering Club Hillwalker's Guide.* Scottish Mountaineering Trust.

Bennet, Donald (ed), *The Corbetts and other Scottish Hills.* Scottish Mountaineering Trust.

Brown: Hamish, *Hamish's Mountain Walk.* Gollancz. *Climbing the Corbetts.* Gollancz.

Dawson, Alan, *The Relative Hills of Britain.* Cicerone Press.

Drummond, Peter, *Scottish Hill and Mountain Names.* Scottish Mountaineering Trust.

McNeish, Cameron, *The Munro Almanac.* Neil Wilson Publishing. *The Best Hillwalking in Scotland.* Neil Wilson Publishing.

Mountaineering Council of Scotland and the Scottish Landowner's Federation, *Heading for the Scottish Hills.* Scottish Mountaineering Trust.

Munro's Tables and other tables of lesser heights. Scottish Mountaineering Trust.

Robertson, Bill, *The Scottish Mountain Guide.* Mainstream Publishing.

Weather Information

Climber and Hillwalker Climblines:
    East Highlands, tel: 0891-654668
    West Highlands, tel: 0891-654669

Weather forecasts for outdoor pursuits are broadcast every weekend on BBC Radio Scotland and avalanche reports appear every day in *The Herald* and *The Scotsman.*

Alphabetical list of Corbetts